# FRENCH WINE UNCORKED

A journey into the cellars and vineyards of France

Neal Atherton

Copyright © 2020 Neal Atherton

All rights reserved

The characters and events portrayed in this book are factual. It is a work of non-fiction and all the places and events are correct to the best of the authors knowledge at the time of visiting.

No part of this book may be reproduced, or stored in a retrieval system, or transmitted in any form or by any means, electronic, mechanical, photocopying, recording, or otherwise, without express written permission of the publisher.

Photography by Neal Atherton

Cover design by: Neal Atherton

*Dedicated to the friends that enjoyed the fruits of our travels and most dearly to those no longer with us*

# CONTENTS

Title Page
Copyright
Dedication
Photography
Introduction
French Wine Uncorked   1
Leaving the shores of England – to France   7
A return to France - Chablis   16
Off the Beaten Track in Northern Burgundy   30
Le Jardin Gourmand   41
The Château and Sancerre   46
Champagne   63
Heading South   74
Chenonceaux and Touraine Wines   100
Burgundy – The Angels Share   118
Beaujolais   139
Maximes   148
Pouilly-Fuissé & the Ebullient M.Roy   157
Rural Burgundy & Beaujolais   171
Collioure and a Catalan Treasure   181
Corbières & Minerverois   188
There is More   200
Domaine Addresses in Book Order   201

| | |
|---|---|
| About The Author | 207 |
| Praise For Author | 209 |
| Books By This Author | 211 |

# PHOTOGRAPHY

**This book has some accompanying photography from the French wine regions and can be viewed on my website : www.nealatherton.com**

link: FRENCH WINE UNCORKED PHOTOGRAPHY

all photography on website copyright Neal Atherton

# INTRODUCTION

In this my fourth book about our travels in France I write about our journey around the vineyards and into the cellars of the French wine regions. The people we met and the places we visited were unforgettable and we made many friends.

As with all my books I do not specifically write them to be guide books. Rather I want to give you a flavour of this wonderful country and inspire you to want to travel and experience France for yourself.

I do however in this book provide contact details for all the producers we visited so you can easily follow in our footsteps. Please enjoy and perhaps sit and read with a chilled glass of Sancerre.

I apologize in advance for the overuse of the word *'terroir'* and sadly I am still unable to give you a definitive definition of this uniquely French term.

# FRENCH WINE UNCORKED

'A bottle of your finest Blue Nun waiter, merci'.

I think that was the extent of my ability to order a bottle of wine back in the 1970's. The only other wine that was swirling around in my consciousness would be Crown of Crowns Liebfraumilch, a wine that at the time seemed to be very exotic. In its own way this was a bottle somewhat like Château Petrus would be today in my aspirations. When one of your dining companions is merrily downing a 'yard of ale' at the bar this era is clearly not a time period when we had any thoughts of being connoisseurs of the vine. Truly though, they were the only two wines that I thought existed and the North of England was not overrun with alternatives. Nor to be fair did I have any thoughts of seeking any out even if they were readily available. Oh, I had forgotten the brief flirtation my future wife and her friends had with Babycham and I do recall an occasional Tia Maria after the end of a restaurant meal. There was also something alcoholic in the Irish coffee that was so ubiquitous following a restaurant meal in the 1970's. However, the days of wine departments in our supermarkets were a very long way into the future.

My knowledge of wine did not improve and my only real encounter with anything more interesting in this unknown world of grape fermentation was when someone bought us a bottle of Barsac, a sweet wine which I now know is produced in one of the communes of the Sauternes appellation in the Gironde region of France. At the time I thought it was a pleasant wine, sweet of course as nobody seemed to drink anything dry even if there was such a thing as a dry wine. That bottle was a gift for our honeymoon in 1979 and quite enjoyable it was but even that did not stir in me a desire to know any more about wine or for that matter drink any more than was really necessary in a social context. It was some years later when we saw a bottle that was vaguely familiar on a supermarket shelf, familiar in the sense that I had heard it mentioned somewhere before. It was a bottle of Moselle, though being German of course it was spelt Mosel. German wines as far as I was aware were the only wines available in Lancashire and I was probably not far wrong in that assumption. These wines always had a certain sweetness to them. So my third variety of wine was tried and I think that as I was now approaching thirty years old I was displaying a shocking lack of knowledge about a subject that would become very interesting and wonderful to me later in life. We did quite like the Mosel so this became our wine of choice for a few years although to be honest we only bought a bottle about once every four weeks when I got paid.

Life in the 1990's got a bit more serious, work was stressful and a lot of responsibility came my way. The children were growing into teenagers and so my life was full and this left me little spare time - except for playing cricket. Funnily enough, despite all the pressures of life, they did not drive me to drink. My knowledge of wine was still very tenuous to say the least. I did not come from a family of drinkers although when I delved into the family history I soon found out that the previous generations more than made up for our tiny consumption, but that is another story. My father had a bottle of Dubonnet, housed in a wicker basket on the living room bookcase and I feel sure this lasted him several years. I cannot recall my mother ever having a glass in her hand. To be honest the subject of wine or any form of alcohol was extremely peripheral to my enjoyment of life and so it remained until one day my wife started a part time evening job around the mid 1990's.

In those days my knowledge of food was also rather limited – no, make that to be exclusively of Lancastrian delicacies and only a select few of those. My diet as it had always been in my formative years was to start the day with a fried English breakfast and go steadily downhill from there. Red meat, chicken if pushed, pies, gravy, fish and chips and by now I am struggling to think of anything else that kept me alive. I never up to this point had eaten an onion, any vegetable other than carrots or peas, certainly no garlic and olive oil was for putting in your ear to soften the wax. I had no idea that fish could be supplied without it being surrounded by batter or that potatoes could be cooked in anything other than lard. Believe me I am not joking and my father is even worse as regards his diet but he has lived to be over ninety – forget that Mediterranean diet.

So one night I was sat alone in front of the TV. That evening I did for some reason watch the English chef Rick Stein in his very first series, focusing of course on his love of fish cookery. This was not my usual choice of viewing, although in those days there still was not much choice anyway, but what impressed me and held my attention was his enthusiasm for his subject. I will generally listen to anyone as long as they enthuse about their subject. As I watched his series I found myself drawn to the realisation that there was a whole new world of interest out there. One thing I noticed, this was more than apparent when he teamed up with his mate Keith Floyd, was that cooking and food seemed to them to require a glass of wine to achieve the desired effect. Nothing else in my life has had more impact on how I view a particular subject than that series of programs. I now wanted to cook and I desired to learn about food and the world of wine. Life was never the same again.

Over the next couple of years I started to cook and especially when Niamh was working. I would try out my new skills on the children and these resulting dishes were all new to me as well. Garlic and olive oil, naked fish, vegetables, rice, noodles, tomatoes, sauces, herbs, ginger and spices – what is going on? I loved them, all of them and I loved following recipes and watching other chefs as the British food scene started to explode and become interesting at last. Chefs like the sadly departed Gary Rhodes made British food not just palatable but almost trendy. But it was the fish cookery of Rick Stein that had the most impact on me as I found that the ingredients I most loved to work with were fish and seafood. Where had they been all my life? What of wine though, how could I learn about that and would it improve my cooking just as it seemed to do with the TV chefs? It would take another leap of faith to find out.

# LEAVING THE SHORES OF ENGLAND – TO FRANCE

In my first book in the French travel series I told the story of how we initially went abroad on holiday – to the South of France close to Perpignan near to the Spanish border. It was here on the splendid camp site of Brasilia at Canet Plage overlooking the Mediterranean that my wine education really began. It was again because of someone that had great enthusiasm for his subject. On the camp site was a small wine cave and the owner was passionate about the wines from the

Roussillon region, the produce of the *terroir* of this sun baked land. I visited him in his shop every morning despite this being a little early for a tasting session. The shop was always quiet at that time of the day and he was willing to talk about the wines of the region as he personally knew the producers whose wines he stocked. Some of these domaines were located nearby and one was within walking distance (just) - Château de l'Esparrou owned and run by the Famille Bonfils on the route de Saint-Cyprien - 66140 Canet en Roussillon. It was at this Château that I made my start to understand the difference in the type of wines that could be produced from essentially the same grapes. My friend in the wine cave and subsequently the friendly owners of the vineyard explained that they were able to produce wines outside of the Appellation d'origine contrôlée, doing so alongside wines that matched the control system specifications. The wines to my palate were very fine, a revelation to someone who had relied on the limited choice available on the shelves back in the UK. It was also starting to fire my interest in the whole subject as well as encouraging me to try a larger variety of wines of course. There is more about Château de l'Esparrou and our wine adventures with them in my first book – FIRST TIME WE SAW PARIS.

At the little shop my friend encouraged me to be more adventurous about the wines I was choosing and his infectious enthusiasm led me into a totally new world of pleasure and interest. One of the wines they are so devoted to in this region is the sweet Rivesaltes wine. In fact, at the Bastille Day celebrations every July 14$^{th}$ the campsite holds a parade and everyone is expected to take a drink, or should I say catch a drink from the long necked carafe that our friend Diego held at arm's length to pour the amber liquid down on you. A fair quantity of the wine ended up on the floor or on your clothes but it was all good fun and another departure from being in my comfort zone. I was learning the culture of French wine very quickly and getting quite immersed and rather obsessed with it. The wine cave on site also sold wines by the petrol pump method and these could be dispensed into five litre containers. It has to be said that I was not yet ready to leap from drinking half a bottle a week to that sort of quantity and it is probably as well that I never would. These wines were incredibly inexpensively priced at around no more than two Euros for a container. What was quite amazing was the quality of these wines emerging from the large stainless tanks. This was also a lesson learned quite early on – wines in France from a small producer or retailer, or indeed a house wine in a restaurant are usually very acceptable indeed. These people will never risk their reputation on selling you a poor bottle or glass of wine. The other lesson that became apparent early on was that the French surely do keep all the best wines at home. Years on from our initial travels you will never convince me that the allegedly same bottle of wine purchased and drunk in the UK is better or equal to the equivalent bottle obtained in France. Perhaps it is just a case of the location producing that effect. I have tried and tried over the years with Sancerre, my wife Niamh's favourite wine, and I cannot get close to the quality in the UK that I can buy in and around that hilltop village.

The man in the shop had very easily and gently given me the confidence to go out into the wine world and explore. First of all this would be in the restaurants of the region. The house wines were fine but I was now feeling that I could experiment a little and start choosing a bottle that I had now become familiar with. Individual village names now started to mean something to me. Inevitably this region inspired a love of rosé wines and these examples produced in the intense sunshine of Languedoc-Roussillon are very fruity and drinkable on a baking hot lunchtime or in fact at any time on a warm sunny Mediterranean day.

Again some of our joyful early experiences of discovering the pleasures of Roussillon wines are in that first book but I must recall our very first visit to a real wine cave when we found ourselves at Cave Tambour, 136 Bis Avenue du Puig del Mas, 66650 Banyuls-sur-Mer. Back then in the late 1990's they had a rather undeveloped tasting room but if you look on-line today you can see that they have taken the visiting experience to a much higher level. I have to say though that one of the joys of tasting wine in France is to be in a rustic setting, tasting fresh from the barrel as it were. Most producers now have taken the 'degustation' to a more clinical and business like experience but there was something quite magical in being able to visit and taste when it seemed that you were a guest at the producers table. Times have changed but the wines are still equally good, it is just that everything seemed to taste better and be more exciting when times were simpler. Yes,

I concede we are getting older.

At Cave Tambour they produce a variety of Banyuls wine, a variety that is naturally sweet and this produces the most delightful of wines that in no way mirror sweet wines that have sugar added. These offer a totally different taste sensation. I love the way the owners express their pride in the method of production, saying that they respect 'des méthodes ancestrales de vinification'. Their ancestors produced the wine in this way and they see no reason to change the method now. If you can seek out such passionate producers in France then you will be richly rewarded and you will probably leave as friends. It would be difficult to choose a favourite wine here at Tambour. Believe me we tried them all, but probably 'Rimage', a wine produced exclusively from the grenache grape would be my choice of the six varieties on offer. Cave Tambour also produces bold red wines under the Collioure appellation but on the day we were there it was the sweet non fortified Banyuls that we were eager to try. Cave Tambour was I think the very first producer that we purchased wine from, closely followed by Château de l'Esparrou. We were learning fast and had a thirst (sorry) for more knowledge and definitely to be taught by means of more tastings. There was one aspect of the production of wine that Niamh and my daughter Charlotte learnt on that visit to the Tambour cellar. It was that 'sweet' does not equate to weak. Sweet Banyuls may be a wine that is very pleasant and immensely quaffable but it does carry a strength that is closely on a par with port - deceptively strong. It was quite amusing to see them pondering the location of the way they came in to the cave when the tasting ended. They were extremely happy with the experience it has to be said.

One other trip we made on those early visits to Languedoc-Roussillon found us in Limoux, a village at the centre of a wine appellation around 25 kilometres south of Carcassonne. The village is famous for the sparkling wine produced here; a wine that they would argue is more than a match for Champagne. Sadly, they are not allowed to refer to this wine as Champagne, although to be fair Champagne cannot call their fizz Limoux. Blanquette de Limoux is the well-known variety and this was the version we tasted and we purchased a few bottles for home. Again this tasting was in an ancient wine cave on the main street - it was a very authentic setting. You feel a great sense of historical and ancestral pride among the producers of this entire region and they were adding to my fascination with the whole subject of wine and its production. I do sense that they would probably not sell a bottle to you if you did not appreciate just how much the product and the legacy behind it meant to them. Blanquette de Limoux certainly is of a quality that would give most Champagne houses a run for their money.

These were the early stirring of a subject that would turn into a passion as we started to tour France more independently but first of all it would be a return to England and a chance to build on this initial knowledge so gratefully received. I could now at least start to look like a genuine wine snob as I wandered down and studied the burgeoning wine aisles of the English supermarkets as they took advantage of the awakening interest in wine brought on by the TV chefs. I was finding a real joy in cooking and pairing wines to go with the food, nothing too deep and meaningful as yet, but just a new found pleasure that I was sure would continue to develop as my understanding grew. I was like a sponge finding and taking in this new knowledge. It would be a return to France that would move my interest on by leaps and bounds but this would not be as an independent traveller. On one of the now multitude of food and travel programs flooding the TV networks there was an item about a travel company – Arblaster & Clarke - who offered wine tours, many of them to France. To say I was captivated would be a real understatement, the details were taken down and next day I was on the phone. I thought this would make a fine anniversary surprise for Niamh and so without any further delay a tour was booked. The one I had chosen was to be a tour of the Loire valley and Northern Burgundy. From this tour I would not only gain some expert knowledge but it would be the wines discovered on this visit that would always be the favourite ones for Niamh and me. It would be our first encounter with Sancerre and Chablis and some lesser known varieties, ones that were unknown in England and would remain so for many years. Let me take you there on this discover, one that is easy to recreate today and I do urge you to make plans to visit this area of delicious and very special wines.

# A RETURN TO FRANCE - CHABLIS

I explained in my first book that my baby steps in foreign travel i.e. France were only taken in 1997 and so at the time of this wine tour I only had three years of experience in travelling abroad and was still a travel novice. I also still felt very Lancastrian, very Northern. Not insecure mind you, but conscious that my accent and outlook could set me apart from my fellow wine travellers. This was indeed the case. We were clearly the only people on the tour from north of the M25 and although Niamh does not speak as if she has just taken a break from the cotton mills, I most certainly do. Certainly at that time there was still a sense that to be overly interested in wine must mean that you are an upper class snob. Although my fellow connoisseurs definitely had a public school façade to their character they were by no means unfriendly or snobbish, far from it. I have to concede that I had to take a fair bit of good natured banter as regards my accent but we would all have a great time together, well most of us anyway. This was an excellent way to go farther out of our comfort zone. This whole experience would give us so much more confidence on our future travels in France as regards touring the vineyards. It would also make us much more gregarious in our dealings with people.

One pleasure in life that has stayed with me really came to the fore on this trip. It was the joy of people watching. It also made me realize that I too would be part of that activity and at the end of this trip I would definitely always take myself much less seriously. The start of the trip from Folkestone by Eurotunnel was uneventful apart from the unusual experience of being inside a coach inside a coach – a can within a can. We made our way down to Auxerre and could not help listening to a bizarre conversation going on between a couple of people sat behind us. They were giving out a lot of criticism about the driver and the route he was taking and getting quite stroppy about it. They were also making what seemed to be very informed suggestions. Today we are all connected to GPRS in some way or another but back then it was not the norm. These two intrepid travellers had a GPRS system with them and were using it to follow every movement of the coach and its driver. It turned out they were both pilots in the RAF and I hoped that the equipment they had with them was not denying a fellow pilot his guidance system. It would be fair to say they were a rather self-absorbed couple who clearly enjoyed taking their work home with them. They used this equipment on every visit we made to the vineyards during the tour and at no time did they ever agree with the driver – perhaps they were just so used to travelling as the crow flies. At no time during the tour do I recall them bonding with anyone in the party but I sense that the feeling was probably mutual – no one was going to burst their bubble.

On this initial tour we stayed at Hotel Normandie, 41 boulevard Vauban, 89000, Auxerre France. It is a hotel that is very conveniently located for strolling around the medieval city of Auxerre. It is also close to towns and wine villages like Chablis, St Bris or even Sancerre. It was an extremely pleasant stay with the only drawback being our having to cross a fairly busy road to start exploring Auxerre and some of the party it has to be said were not as young as they used to be.

Our first visit of the tour is indeed to Chablis and the domaine that starts the tour would become one of our very favourite producers in the years to come. This was perhaps the real start to our wine education, a time where we could have first-hand knowledge of the production process, the traditions of the producers. We would receive a sort of explanation of the French word *'terroir'* although it does not readily convert into English. We would see the soil and the vines and in the case of the vineyards producing Chablis this was an eye opener. When I think of the word soil I imagine; well soil really, but that is not the word I would use to describe where the vines of Chablis are planted. Perhaps it is *terroir*. The 'soil' is really a very gravely, mineral mix, a concoction more likely to be seen on a building site or road construction. The French call it – Kimméridgien. The stones are a fossil mix, mainly oysters mixed with the clay soil and it is astonishing to see anything growing here, being able to take root in such a loose mix of stone and dry 'soil'. The land and location are difficult to work and the climate can be unforgiving. Over the years many different methods of warding off the regular late spring frosts have been employed and in the past the sight of braziers in the vineyards was common. Times moved on to oil and propane heaters and more modern methods. For the long suffering producers here in Chablis spring always brings a gamble with the weather and much production can be lost with sudden frosts. The producers of Chablis will tell you that the mixture of minerals and the local climate are what you can taste when they have worked their magic on the chardonnay vines. What you cannot argue is that the taste of Chablis is unmistakable and unique and must be linked to the *terroir* of this small wine region. The finest Chablis vineyards are spread out on the slopes that curve and wrap around the town. The situation of Chablis, despite the challenges, is perfectly placed for producing this distinctive wine. The vineyards here are classified rigidly according to their status. As you taste from various producers the wines within the classifications from great growths ie Grand Cru down to Petit Chablis you are fully aware of the distinctiveness that is produced by location and differences in the soil. As we will discover on our travels the wines of Chablis although made from chardonnay just like the white Burgundies of the Cote D'Or to the south are very different in character and taste. We quickly come to realise that this will be one of the great pleasures of touring France, discovering how winemakers deal with the conditions they have been dealt and enjoying the differences in character. This is becoming a new hobby and a most enjoyable one.

The town of Chablis is located around 170 kilometres south east of Paris and the land is home to the northernmost vineyards of Burgundy. Chablis is small – using the description of one of its wines you could say it is indeed Petit Chablis. The vineyards are located quite close to the town itself and prior to approaching the town the scenery is one of trees and grazing cattle. It is a town that despite its size is not short of confidence as the wines on offer here can be very fine. Many producers have grown in size and reputation to the extent that their outlets are not shops but must be classed as boutiques. Chablis is a town that is a delightful mix of ancient and modern, the old town is well maintained and its character fully preserved, supported by the money that is brought to the town by the wine production. The town has a mixture of upmarket shops and wine outlets, some fine restaurants but also the more modest local shops and bar/bistro restaurants you expect to find in rural France. There is something for everyone. On Sunday mornings a large and lively market spreads out with stalls throughout the old town and if you are in the area and especially if you are self-catering then you really have to be there. Much of the market is devoted to food stalls and on the day of the market produce from local producers of the surrounding area floods into the town.

As you stroll around the market it soon becomes clear which stalls are the most popular as you observe the locals carrying their shopping bags and baskets making their way to queue for their favourites. These will always include a local cheese producer, a stall selling chickens roasting on a spit with the juices falling onto golden potatoes cooking in the tray below. Rather disconcertingly the stall that wins by a country mile the prize for the most in demand is one producing and selling on site a local blood sausage. It is not a pretty sight. To one side of the stall they are mixing, shaping and boiling the sausages and there is a lot of blood. It is all very medieval which is really in keeping with the town itself.

Near the river Serein at the Quay Voltaire the river splits and a small gently flowing tributary leads under the bridge. You can follow the footpath alongside the banks of the stream.

This is a very attractive spot and the flower filled bank leads down towards the Hôtel Du Vieux Moulin at the far end. From this path you can head back into the winding streets of the town and really explore the medieval architecture. You will pass at least four wine caves representing local producers before you come to the Catholic church of Collégiale Saint-Martin à Chablis, said to be founded in the ninth century with much of the present structure dating from around the $12^{th}$ century.

Also in the town is a Jewish synagogue which is a slightly unexpected discovery but it is actually located on the aptly named Rue des Juifs. This testifies to a longstanding Jewish population in the region going back many centuries. The building tends to be open and you can go inside, just knock if it appears closed.

Going back to our starting point by the bridge

over the River Serein there is located just over the bridge one of the best of the Chablis producers. It is one with a fine tradition and a name that I came across in an old book about French wine (Wines of France) by the wine writer and domaine owner Alexis Lichine. This is Domaine Servin, 20 Avenue Oberwesel, 89800 Chablis. The wine book that I found in an antique shop dates from the 1950's and being a lover of history this step back in time to the vineyards in France was very atmospheric and certainly pre-dates the more technological and clinical approach to wine production today. Perhaps I could quote a passage that really encapsulates the story of the wines and people of Chablis and gives a hint of the *terroir* and tradition and all that means:

"Servin is a stocky, moustached man in his sixties, who wears felt slippers in the house and wooden sabots (type of clog) when he goes out of doors, dressed in corduroys the colour of ripe olives when new and the colour of dried ripe olives when old. Although many vineyard workers now wear rubber boots, Servin clings to the heavy wooden clogs that used to typify the peasant.

His son is a polite, cheerful smiling boy in his thirties. His wife is a grey-haired pretty woman.

With them lives his father, who is ninety three, has a hearty wheeze, is bent double from working among the vines all his life, and, with nine decades of knowing it behind him, strains the hard, white wine of Chablis through his yellow moustache. On good days he still does some pottering about the vineyard."

The life of a winemaker was a hard one back then and still is a gamble on the weather today but production methods have moved on as we will see, and the Domaine Servin is also now an example of modernity. Chablis is a prosperous town and the promotion of its fine wines is generally now very slick and professional.

The first encounter we were to have with Chablis wine was really throwing us in at the deep end as it was to be to one of the most respected producers of Chablis - Domaine Laroche, whose boutique is at 10, rue Auxerroise 89800 CHABLIS. This is definitely a boutique rather than a simple wine outlet and it testifies to the quality of the fine wines that Laroche is famous for. They produce the full range of Chablis right up to Grand Crus and they also have a domaine in the Languedoc region. Those southern wines are also available here in Chablis. Their wines are exceptional and the prices can reflect that with the Grand Cru wines being over 100 Euros a bottle even when purchased from the domaine. Laroche have many parcels of land in the Chablis appellation and you can indulge yourself with virtually all the well-known versions of this beautiful mineral wine. Premier Cru Les Fourchaumes is one that really impressed but this is definitely a bottle to be saved for a special occasion.

The lady that took us through the very generous tasting was exquisitely dressed and presented. She knew her subject well and was proud of the long traditions of Laroche. In some ways this was an intimidating introduction to our wine lessons; it felt a quite special and exclusive place to be and certainly increased our expectation for what was in store for us in this region. The atmosphere in the tasting room lightened up after a few glasses and felt a lot more comfortable. We finally broke away from the tasting and we were all taken through the narrow streets of the town to a very ancient place that Laroche are still using to age their wines. The Obédiencerie is a building steeped in Chablis history and tradition. The canons of St Martin, who settled Chablis, were the most important winemakers and cultivators of vines down through the centuries, from the middle ages right up until the French Revolution. Here there is a massive ancient wooden wine press and it is a spectacular sight in the old wooden beamed room – wine making history is right before your eyes making a feast for the imagination. The heavy beams that give weight to the press are enormous and would have been felled from a huge oak tree from the surrounding forests many centuries ago. These beams are worked by a most precise wooden corkscrew that again was hewn out of a large ancient timber. It is quite a sight and a mesmerising end to our visit.

The visit was all very enjoyable and took me far outside my personal comfort zone. A wine boutique such as this one here in Chablis at Laroche does not exist in the North of England. Although many in the party were used to such a splendid environment in which to taste wine this was all another world to me but I have to say one that I could quickly become accustomed to. The next tasting just outside of Chablis would be more suited to my Lancashire peasant status but very fine nonetheless.

The subsequent Chablis producer to play host to our merry and varied band of wine lovers is Domaine Alain Geoffroy, 4 rue de l'équerre 89800 Beine (Près(near) Chablis). We will return to the domaine of M.Geoffrey repeatedly over the coming years with an empty boot in our car.

Alain and his team produce Chablis ranging from the modest Petit Chablis right up to Grand Cru status and they are all particularly fine examples created in the true tradition of Chablis. It is that taste, that *terroir* that comes through and for us novices in French wine these are a revelation, so unlike and so superior to anything we have ever tasted back in England. We are in awe and as the generous tasting extends to around six or seven examples the noise in the vaulted tasting room grows ever more in intensity and the atmosphere is lively and joyous. We may on the surface be quite reserved as English but we loosen up remarkably well over a glass or two or three. My personal favourite of the Chablis versions on offer would be Chablis 1er Cru Fourchaume, a wine from relatively old vines although not as old as the Vieilles Vignes example. This meets the Appellation Chablis Premier Cru Contrôlée to perfection and will keep and mature superbly for around 10 years.

The tasting cellar here at Domaine Geoffrey is beautiful, covered by a vaulted stone ceiling held up by solid ancient pillars. The acoustics after a glass or two of wine are remarkable. The domaine itself dates back to around 1850 and was founded by a descendant of the family Honoré Geoffroy but it is the present generation that have taken the house to a much higher level and presence in the Chablis region. New stainless steel tanks are used for producing all the chardonnay wines except for the Vieilles Vignes which are still allocated to wooden barrels. The welcome is warm and generous and we leave with a pallet load of cases consigned to the cavernous boot of the coach. This visit has made a tremendous impression and increased my thirst for more wine knowledge and experiences. This is to be a short tour but will give us an excellent foundation for our future travel and interest in the world of French wines. It is a happy place to be.

# OFF THE BEATEN TRACK IN NORTHERN BURGUNDY

In the evening we started to learn an important lesson in our French wine education. That lesson was always to take the time to explore a little farther than producers that are familiar or well known. This would be to search outside the famous villages such as Chablis and seek out independent producers, many of which would be quite small operations. To our hotel that evening the tour company had arranged for one such producer to bring a selection of his wines and we would be given a tasting in the comfort of the hotel. This up and coming producer was Emmanuel Dampt from the village of Collan, NW of Chablis. Emmanuel came with his young son, Theo, a boy aged around eight years old who served as his sommelier for the evening. Dampt was not a name that anyone was familiar with in our party. At that time I don't think they exported to the UK but since that evening they have gone from strength to strength.

We had a very convivial evening and our wine guide translated and explained the method and *terroir* that held the key to producing the wines. The domaine consists of three brothers who took over the business their father started around 1980. Emmanuel is a very modest man and unassuming about his wines which he has no reason to be as they are superb in every respect. The domaine has been responsible for reviving the Tonnerre appellation, planting chardonnay once more in a location that had fallen into disuse. This has given birth to an excellent Chablis alternative. Alongside the various Chablis examples that they produce from assorted parcels of land located within the appellation they have a very fine and interesting range of wines.

The next day we set out for their domaine in

Collan to learn more, of course to have another tasting, but especially to buy some of their wines to take back to the UK. Emmanuel and his wife would also provide us with lunch on long trestle tables right alongside their vats and barrels in the domaine. Everyone was absorbed in the special moment that this provided, generous rustic fare complemented by a seemingly endless supply of superb wines. The sweet aroma of the 'Angel's share' was wafting through the cellar, one of life's great pleasures. The wines from the Dampt domaine, and this is generally true of most independent producers, have a certain something about them that the larger more well-known establishments cannot replicate.

Although people like the Dampts have to adhere to the requirements of the appellation specification they seem to be able to express themselves with more freedom producing wines that are incomparable with anything we can find in the North of England. For instance they produce a remarkable wine called Chevalier D'Eon which is a white Bourgogne Tonnerre produced to that appellation specification. This becomes our 'house wine' in the years to come and for anyone who loves a good Chablis this is one you must try, similar to Chablis but distinctively of the Tonnerre *terroir*. It also is named after the most remarkable man (or woman) Charles d' Eon de Beaumont who was of dubious gender. He was used by Louis XVI as a spy, chiefly to Russia, where he worked as a woman. In fact Louis always thought that he was a woman and when he finally came to spend more time back in Tonerre cultivating his vineyards Louis insisted that he live as a woman - Mademoiselle la Chevalière d'Eon. He had to return to England to settle some affairs but fell foul of the Revolution occurring in France in his absence, losing his Royal patronage and allowance as well as his land holdings. He made a reasonable living by taking part in fencing competitions but eventually is badly injured and dies in London. His post mortem pronounces him a man. So if you buy a bottle of this named chardonnay from Emmanuel then remember the story – the label shows Chevalière d'Eon dressed appropriately in half and half costume.

The range of Chablis is excellent and some are expertly produced by another of the Dampt brothers – Eric. They have some very old vines that provide the grapes for the Chablis Vieilles Vignes and this is well worth seeking out. Perhaps the very best reason for going off the beaten track is to be found in the wonderful fizz that they produce here in the Tonnerre region – Crémant De Bourgogne. Here in Northern Burgundy we are close to the Champagne region but even if you are only five hundred yards away you cannot call a wine Champagne. However I defy anyone to try a bottle without knowing its origin and not pronounce it to be fine Champagne. It is that good and a fraction of the price of any named Champagne and worth the drive here for this wine alone.

The Dampt family are warm and welcoming. Not only have we learned a lot more about the wines of the region and seen the method of production but as we watch Emmanuel with his forklift truck bring out a full laden heavy pallet of cases of wine we know we have much to enjoy when we return home.

For our next visit we again stayed off the beaten track and it was to a village that has become much more known in the UK for its lovely wines but at the time I doubt that it would have caused a small ripple of acknowledgement to even the most ardent lover of the regions wines. This visit was a surprise to me and a very enjoyable one at that and also one that was a great relief to my wallet – it was to the village of Saint Bris. The domaine is - Domaine Bersan, Jean-Louis & Jean-Christophe, 20, rue du Docteur Tardieux, 89530 Saint-Bris-le-Vineux. There is another Bersan domaine on the same street but their wines are the ones we sampled. Saint Bris is a very ancient wine village and dates back to around the 15$^{th}$ century as regards wine production and it is here that you really do have the best of all worlds, a village that can provide a most acceptable alternative to Chablis but also a sauvignon blanc to rival Sancerre. Not forgetting the fine Irancy red wine that is a lovely light pinot noir in the style expected of Northern Burgundy. One wine we were offered for tasting, and it would be a bottle I would look for in the future in restaurants in Northern Burgundy, was Bourgogne Côtes d'Auxerre chardonnay, a white wine I have never seen in the UK. It is a small production but even so it is so good that I am surprised it is not better known. It is all here and Saint Bris was one of the best discoveries on this tour and a place that we would gladly return to in the years to come. The tasting once again was generous and the Saint Bris sauvignon the favourite of all with many bottles from the range being purchased. The boot of the coach was becoming exceedingly full.

The village of Saint Bris has the most extensive cellars and tunnels stretching for miles under the entire village. These were dug out and made secure as far back as the 11$^{th}$ century and their original purpose was as a safeguard for the town against marauding enemies. They seem to meander endlessly under the area but on this group visit our tasting was above ground. Consequently we did not get to see the cellars below as time was pressing as the tastings always seem to overrun. It was not for about four years or so before we had the opportunity to return to see the Bersan domaine but on that later occasion the tasting we were treated to by these very friendly wine makers Jean-Louis and Jean-Christophe was very much below ground. Let me just expand then a little more on what can be found in this delightful village and especially at the Domaine Bersan.

You enter the cellars through an opening where the barrels are rolled into the cellar down some ancient stone steps. All the time minding your head as you pass through the narrow entrance. Jean-Louis took us well into the ancient vaulted cellars until finally around another corner there was an oak barrel, the top prepared with glasses. Next to the barrel there was a refrigerator – how do they get electricity down here? It has to be said that the cellars are not very high and they do go on and on for miles. So if you have any tendency towards claustrophobia then I am quite sure that this experience is just not for you I am afraid. The tasting on our solo visit was again very generous and given added spice by the location deep under the village. M.Bersan asked if I would like to explore further into the dark, narrow passageways and into the multitude of side corridors. I was excited to do so but Niamh was not willing to go farther and I felt a little guilty at leaving her alone but at least she had plenty of wine in the fridge to calm the nerves.

On this later visit to Saint Bris and Domaine Bersan we were so impressed with the wines on offer that we purchased from right across the range and the car was getting quite full. The wines here are of such incredible value for the quality that it is an irresistible collection of wines that makes it difficult to choose just one or two. They produce an Aligote white wine here and this is rarely seen in the UK. I concede that it is not to everyone's taste but we found it was a lovely wine to serve with food and particularly with cheese. Aligote is quite floral and fresh. It is certainly a wine that is worth a case to see if it translates its character without compromise back home in England. We purchased two white Saint Bris, one case of the vieilles vignes from vines that are around fifty years old and two cases of the classic Saint Bris. Both are lively and fresh wines and so typical of the village because they can only be produced from vines in and around the village itself. Hence the production is small and although you can find this wine in the UK it is definitely a wine that repays you for buying at the source.

As previously mentioned here at Bersan they also produce the rare Burgundy Côtes d'Auxerre Blanc and we found this to be a special find on our travels. I have never seen a bottle in the UK and the production is tiny. In Burgundy of course the wine variety is generally chardonnay and as you travel from north to south in that region you will find many different examples of white Burgundy right up to the stellar bottles of the Grand Crus. Auxerre is more modest but it is a rich aromatic wine, perhaps slightly nutty in character from the minerality of the soil. I think this would be a great wine to enjoy with that speciality of Burgundy - jambon persillé, a ham terrine with plenty of parsley. This is a dish I have tried to recreate many times but never quite captured the version offered here at source. Once again this is a delightful discovery here in Northern Burgundy.

The variety of wines produced here at Bersan extends to a range of Chablis. Their Chablis comes from vines that are located in the village of Préhy, growing as to be expected on Kimmeridgian soils. It is a lively Chablis and has a citrus edge to it. It is a good solid example that compares well with offerings available over in Chablis itself. Finally we bought the red Irancy, a wine that most people in the UK would be unfamiliar with but now starting to become a little better known. The grape variety is 95% pinot noir which is what you would expect of a red burgundy and also 5% of a rarely used vine called césar (ceasar). As you would expect of Northern Burgundy it is a light red wine and goes very well with chicken or cold meats. It is a delight with a fine cheese board and you will always find one of those in this region.

We did very well here and have not left much room for many more bottles but I am sure we managed to squeeze many more into the car somehow.

Anyway, let's go back a few years once more to our group visit and for now we can have a rest from tasting and look forward to a meal together.

This evening we have a group meal booked at one of Auxerre finest restaurants located just over the road from our hotel. It was so close that even our RAF guidance system would not be needed tonight. It would provide for us one of the most memorable occasions we would ever have in France.

# LE JARDIN GOURMAND

Even after all these years this ancient town house restaurant in Auxerre has to be the very best dining experience Niamh and I have ever had in France. Maybe not the absolute best from a cooking standpoint, but I split hairs here, definitely the very best all round experience without any doubt. Let me try if I can to describe that evening on our wine tour, an evening when the party consisted of like-minded wine tourists who were determined to soak up every last drop of the French dining experience on offer tonight.

It is a short stroll across Boulevard Vauban to number 56 - Le Jardin Gourmand. The beautiful shaded garden gives off a gorgeous fragrance on this warm still evening as our happy party of twenty or so funnel into the restaurant for our reserved meal. The welcome is warm and inviting and the first delight is seeing the large round communal table perfectly set out, gorgeous flower table settings around which there is gleaming cutlery on perfect white table cloths. We are shown to our table and each person eased into his or her chair with such gentle kindness. The host for our evening of joy can only be described as the most caring and tender of hosts. If you know the US series Frazier then in appearance he is Niles to an absolute tee. An uncanny likeness. His mannerisms also are so like Niles that it feels quite surreal. His attention to detail is astonishing and his one thought is to ensure that we will leave having had the very best of experiences in his restaurant.

In our party was a profoundly deaf lady who everyone (except two) took a lot of care over and made sure that she got full benefit from the tastings and meals. We had got quite fond of her as she was a lovely lady who did not demand anything extra because of her disability. The maître d' was so kind with her and came up very close to her and read the entire menu making sure that she understood, even translating the French expressions. She was very moved by his kindness and we were most impressed with his level of care and service. We also had a lady in our group that was quite restricted in her mobility and again he went out of his way to ensure that she was comfortable at the table. All this attention before we had ordered any food – extraordinary!

The meal itself took nearly four hours as course after course including the usual pre- starters, pre-mains, pre-desserts and petit fours came and were enjoyed. Each course was paired with specific wines, so the lamb would have a Northern Burgundy red pinot noir, the fish course of beautiful John Dory perhaps a white Bourgogne Côtes d'Auxerre. Cheese would be complimented by a Bourgogne Red or a white Aligote. The dessert experience would be accompanied by a smooth desert wine or if you wish a Marc de Champagne. Coffee to finish of course.

That is just a summary and I am sure you would not want me to describe in detail every morsel we ate that evening. I would rather you gained just a flavour of the atmosphere of warmth and determination to please which when accompanied with astoundingly excellent cooking and the best of ingredients adds up to the most memorable of evenings.

Just to pass on to you a particular example of the level and type of service from 'Niles' that actually involved myself. I had become a source of some amusement regarding by lack of adventure when it came to choosing a French cheese. I tended to stick to something that looked more like a Chedder cheese, a familiar texture to me from back home, rather than anything runny or even something as pungent as an Epoisses de Borgogne which I am led to believe is banned on the Paris Metro so that you have to have it delivered!

Our wonderful maître d' even after hours of service giving full attention to our table had observed that I had this mental block as regards the cheese choice. I could see across the restaurant that he had the most incredible cheese trolley or chariot as they like to call them, loaded with every possible variety of cheese from the French regions. He beckoned me from my seat and led me over to the trolley and proceeded to go through every cheese that he felt I should try and would be able to do so without any reservation as to the taste or texture. His descriptions were so engaging that I felt I could put full trust in what he was saying about the character of each cheese and he proceeded to make a personal selection for me. I suppose it was similar to when someone has a personal shopper and that shopper gets everything just right because they have comprehended everything about your tastes and preferences. He got it absolutely correct and not only that he opened up my taste buds for the future and no longer was I going to be so tentative when faced with a French cheese trolley and its proud owner. A truly extraordinary level of service and what made it more so was that you were absolutely sure that he would do the same for everyone in the party if it was required. I sat down very happily but also a little embarrassed at my earlier lack of faith in the selections on offer.

We finally concluded the feast and a very contented party tentatively crossed the road, hesitantly looking both ways before falling into a freshly made inviting bed, ready, well nearly, for the next day's tastings.

It had been a wonderful day. Not only had we visited some excellent wine producers in the area who generously gave of their time and produce, we had concluded at around midnight, a most extraordinary meal served by a true gentleman and an experience that would live not just for a long time in the memory but forever.

# THE CHÂTEAU AND SANCERRE

Next day the morning was bright and clear, a beautiful warm day and perfect weather for the special tasting we had in store. This was the visit we had really been looking forward to – Sancerre and Pouilly sur Loire. It is around ninety five kilometres to Sancerre from Auxerre and the journey took us around an hour and a half. The scenery across to Sancerre is pleasant and the first view of the hilltop wine community of Sancerre is a stunning sight that fills us with anticipation. Around the hilltop vantage point are the regions vineyards stretching out over the rolling hillside, picture perfect in every way. Sancerre is set in a location that unusually gives a view of the entire wine producing vineyards of the appellation from its high viewpoint. The view from the base of the château stretches out in a vast panorama down the slopes to the vineyards of Pouilly and over a large area of the Loire valley. The trains far below pass through the landscape and over the bridges, appearing to be in a model railway landscape. It is one of the finest views in France, particularly if you are a wine lover.

Sancerre is a town that has a long and turbulent past. With its strategic position overlooking the River Loire it could in more violent times take control of the surrounding area. It became a prosperous merchant town that was often at odds with the French king. The town was resolutely Protestant and that caused conflict with the Crown and Sancerre was twice besieged by the Royal armies. The château that features on the labels of some wine bottles is now just a ruined tower dating from the 12$^{th}$ century – Tour des Fiefs. It suffered greatly in times past mainly at the hands of the French King's men. The town was fully in tune with the French Revolution and later one of Napoleon's generals settled here. Interestingly he was called MacDonald and he was Flora MacDonald's nephew. There are many descendants of Scottish settlers living in the area and the famous Château de Tracey is home to a long line that traces its heritage to north of the English border. My wife Niamh's tartan is MacDonald and Sancerre is her most favourite of wine so it must be in the DNA.

Sancerre is now a most peaceful location at the heart of which is a pretty town square with many picturesque streets and alleyways leading into other smaller squares. In one larger square housing the town hall we found the smallest market in France – one fruit and vegetable stall, quite a contrast to the normally bustling markets in the towns and villages of France. The fine town houses of the merchants of Sancerre testify to the wealth that was and still is congregated in this region. Interestingly these houses in the old town were not originally financed by wine but by the wool trade. It is a simple matter to find a good restaurant here and the town also houses many delightful art and craft shops and of course like any self-respecting French town boasts a fine patisserie.

The land around the town is similar in construction to Chablis in that it is made up mainly of limestone and clay. As the consistency varies from vineyard to vineyard the soil produces a different example of the wine in every case. The land with the greater limestone content is the most prized and just as in Chablis the effect of the different *terroir* is very apparent. You will soon discover your favourite expression of Sancerre. Most of the vineyards are south facing and the appellation consists of fourteen communes surrounding the town and also located in the adjacent valleys. The wines are mostly white and this is a well-balanced acidic wine, not overly complex and for a beginner discovering the wines of France it is a great place to start as Sancerre wine gives immediate satisfaction. Once tried Sancerre will become a firm favourite. It is a wine that must be drunk young and we have found that once opened the bottle must be finished. Generally that is never a problem. Sancerre is a wine that is prefect on a hot summer's day as an aperitif but really comes into its own when consumed with fish and seafood. It is a wine that you will find on restaurant menus throughout France and is a reliable choice to make. White wine production dominates and the red and rosé production only accounts for around 20% of the total output of Sancerre.

Our wine tasting visit is to be just north of Sancerre itself at Domaine Laporte, Cave de la Cresle - Route de Sury en Vaux, 18300 Sancerre, Saint Satur. Again the welcome is warm and as is always the case the producers enthusiasm and pride in their wines shines through.

There are some really excellent examples of sauvignon blanc from various parts of the world especially New Zealand but there truly is nothing to compare with the finest expressions of it tasted on site in and around this special village. The essential difficulty of writing a book like this is that I cannot perfectly convey to you just what that taste is like and even if I encourage you to go out and buy a bottle in the UK or US or in fact anywhere outside of this region I know it will not taste exactly as it does in situ, in its *terroir*. I accept that in theory it should not make any difference but it genuinely does. My initial thoughts were that the French do not send the best of the examples outside of the country but it surely is back to this indefinable word of *terroir*, a word that covers so much of the experience of producing and tasting wine. The character of the vineyards of a region seems to seep through to the opened bottle on the table of the restaurant you are dining at, into the food that accompanies the wine. It also seeps into the cellar where you taste the wine with the producer. Particularly is this true of Sancerre and the surrounding villages. I have bought Sancerre many times in the UK and even stretched the budget way beyond what I would normally pay for a bottle just to try to reproduce that sensation of the aroma and the taste of the fresh, vibrant, flinty, gooseberry, acidic white wine but I cannot, it never taste the same. You get an initial sensation of it on first opening a bottle and taking that first taste but it does not linger, it falls flat and I can only put that down to the all-encompassing *'terroir'*. You have to be there, you have to taste Sancerre in and around the village. It is a very special experience.

Domaine Laporte produces many fine wines and I would pick out the Le Rochoy example as my personal favourite. Again the noise levels rise in the tasting room as the generous tasting progresses and the coach is loaded up once again for supplies to be taken back to the UK. We are not finished with Sancerre and today we will have the chance to partake of the white Sancerre that will become our personal favourite and a wine and place we shall return to many times in the years to come.

The coach winds its slow way up the steep sided slopes of the village of Sancerre and your eye is drawn up to the very top of the village along the winding streets leading to the square at its centre. The walk for the final distance provides a breath taking view of the surrounding countryside spread out before you in the plain of the Loire. It is a view that has much fascinating detail to observe as your eye scans the vista from horizon to horizon. It is a beautiful region to absorb from this height. As you emerge into the square at the summit of the village, the Restaurant de la Tour at the gateway, you very much sense that you are in a French village that is devoted to the pleasures of food and wine. In this you will not be disappointed. You will have already as you passed through the gateway to the square seen the wine outlet for the Domaine Alphose Mellot, the window laden with examples of the varieties of Sancerre from the many different parcels of land around the village. It is however the wines and the food from another branch of the family that we will become familiar with today and this first experience of pairing Sancerre wine with food will become an often repeated pleasure over time. Taking up a large part of one side of the square on the left as you enter is the Auberge Joseph Mellot. It is here where we will have lunch as a large party of twenty five or so and it will be an eye opening experience into the world of French food and wine for our still quite novice palates. I feel it is here that our love of French wine and food really deepens and where we begin to develop a real knowledge and understanding of what France has to offer the curious tourist who is willing to learn.

This auberge has been run by the wine making Mellot family for over 130 years and numbers Claude Monet as a customer during that time and I am sure he was not disappointed. The auberge is traditionally decorated inside, an authentic auberge of rural France. Dark wood is everywhere including the tables that are arranged traditionally with modest tablecloths. Pots and pans, paintings, old notices and antique finds including an old copper still adorn virtually every space around the walls. You observe as you enter that a long wooden bar takes up the the left hand side of the room. On an old wooden sideboard are lined up the wines of the domaine, each one named and explained for you and hopefully to encourage you to go to the wine boutique later and take a case or two back home. The history of this wine domaine stretches back around 500 years but it is in more recent times that it has developed into such an important producer in the region. The vineyards and domaine have expanded in recent times under the stewardship of Alexandre Mellot who tragically died quite young in 2005 shortly after our visit. His wife Catherine has carried on his pioneering modernising enterprise since that time. The auberge has always been run by the women of the family and is currently the domaine of Alexandre's sister although on the occasion of our visit it would have been his mother that was in charge and I suspect no one was going to take that privilege away from her as long as she could be there every day.

We were greeted by this formidable lady, and I say that without implying that she was in any way unwelcoming, it was meant in the sense that she was in complete control of this operation. She clearly had standards to maintain and those standards were very high. She effortlessly had us all seated at the prepared tables and had control of the entire service, directing the limited number of waiting staff with the air of a conductor of an orchestra or in this case maybe a string quartet. Something that was unmistakable was her pride in the family auberge, the awareness of carrying on an historical tradition and a sense that she knew that this region, her region, was the finest in all of France. No one, I am sure, was prepared to argue with her.

The food was exceptional, especially in view of the numbers that had to be served. We started with a coarse pate made from local ingredients and this was followed by Oeufs en meurette, a dish that opened up my taste buds to the possibilities available in this bountiful region. The dish consists of eggs poached in what is essentially a Bourgogne sauce, rich in red wine. It was delicious and a revelation, a recipe I would endeavour to repeat as soon as we returned home. A gorgeous chicken dish in a delicate cream sauce followed, the meat falling effortlessly from the bone. Simple country cooking that maximised the taste of the few ingredients that the dish contained. The star of the show however, and this verdict comes from a diner that generally prefers the savoury courses, was the dessert. It was the most exquisite dish of poached pears in red wine, a taste sensation that still lives on in the memory. The key to the success of this dish was that the wine used was from the region, from the Mellot domaine. I often in my cooking shy away from using expensive wine for a sauce or when cooking meat but as we are so often told by chefs who should know – if a wine is not good enough for you to want to drink then you should not cook with it.

The meal was important and meaningful for another reason, well two in fact. One was the way that the wine was utilised to play just as important a part as the food in the enjoyment of the meal. We appreciated the realisation that a wine type, in this case Sancerre, can be so varied when it is produced from grapes from different villages and even fields. This new knowledge would stand us in good stead when we started to tour France on our own and visit vineyards in many parts of the country. The other, and this was more for the benefit of my wife Niamh, was the first encounter with goats cheese. In this case the example served at the end of the meal was the Crottin de Chavignol which is the most famous goat cheese of the many varieties produced in the Loire Valley region. Crottin de Chavignol is a piquant example of goats cheese and totally distinctive. It is a cheese at its best when eaten locally accompanied with the wines of the region. Chavignol village is just a few kilometres from Sancerre as you head back down the slopes and over the plain below. It is a village that also holds claim to have one of the very best parcels of land for producing Sancerre wine. We would in fact visit the commune in later years, mainly for the purpose of buying the crottins of goats cheese but ending up discovering a wonderful Sancerre producer right in the heart of the tiny village. The lunch in the Mellot auberge was a meal of discovery, eye opening in a most wonderful way. I feel that from this lunch we took so much away with us that the desire to learn more and experience the world of French wine became irresistible from that moment on.

By the way, if I have to choose a recommendation for you if you are fortunate enough to find yourself in the village of Sancerre and seated at madam's table it would be La Grande Châtelaine - Cuvée Prestige but please try them all.

The day however was still young despite already having enjoyed around eight or nine Sancerre wines from the morning tasting and the lunch at the auberge. The afternoon visit that would test our stamina and capacity for wine was to be a real treat as we were to visit a fairytale château down in the plain below at the domaine of de Ladoucette - Château du Nozet, 58150 Pouilly-sur-Loire. Baron Patrick de Ladoucette, the current member of the family that own this gorgeous château keeps up the family tradition of producing the most exceptional wines and of course with a concentration on the famous vineyards of Pouilly Fumé. These are vineyards that started to be cultivated for prestigious wines at the end of the 18$^{th}$ century by the family of the Comte Lafond. The Baron keeps that name alive on the bottles of some of his production. Pouilly Fumé is a smaller production than Sancerre and the wines are fairly similar in taste. It is fair to say that this château has been foremost over the decades amongst the producers of the fine wines of this appellation.

The fine examples of Pouilly Fumé could be said to be slightly more complex wines than Sancerre and can be kept a little longer in the bottle. The wines here can have a beautiful long finish, a little more flowery than Sancerre. The main vineyards producing Pouilly Fumé are located around the village of Saint Andelain. A good bottle of Pouilly Fumé can also command a higher price than Sancerre - so be warned. The production is limited by the size of the appellation and the relatively small production allied with the exceptional quality of the wine makes for some eye watering prices for the finest examples. The ability to mature the wine a little more than Sancerre also adds to its appeal as a slightly more complex wine. It is not a wine to be confused with its neighbour Pouilly sur Loire which is a pleasant wine but not in the same class as Pouilly Fumé .

Adding to the rarity value of Pouilly Fumé are the problems the producers have with the location. It is not as protected as the Sancerre vineyards and it can be badly affected by that weather curse that afflicts Northern Burgundy and the Loire – hail. It is not destructive every year but late hail storms cause much damage to the young grapes and this must be a fear that the growers have hanging over them each growing season.

Arriving at Château de Nozet, the home of Baron Patrick Ladoucette you head down the manicured driveway taking in the formal gardens around the château leading into this other land of history and stunning architecture. Our wine education is taking us in a direction of which I certainly had no comprehension - that wine production could exist in such a form. This is a magical place, my granddaughter Ronelle would certainly think that a Disney princess would be certain to emerge from one of the top floor windows and wave us a welcome. It also oozes a sense of wealth and prestige.

The tasting room is quite small but immaculately presented but we will return to that only after a tour of the production area - this is quite a surprise. You initially walk through a narrow passageway that on either side has what appear to be two solid and perfectly straight walls. These are in fact storage tanks set into the concrete containing thousands of gallons of wine in production. Backing these up are more familiar stainless steel tanks emphasizing that this is a very modern and efficient operation that no one could accuse of being stuck in the past. Back at the tasting room it soon becomes clear that however modern the facility may be the wines themselves are a true reflection of the wine tradition of the area and of this particular land around the château. The vineyards come right up to the garden area and the estate is large and bountiful. The favourite wine here has to be the de Ladoucette Pouilly Fumé, unquestionably one of the world's great sauvignon wines. Not to be overlooked though are their Sancerre wines and the domaine also produce a red and rosé wine with the heritage of the Comte Lafonde name. The wine of La Poussie reveals a sweet and enchanting rosé Sancerre from pinot noir grapes and this is a perfect summer aperitif. Ladoucette also has many other domaines that come under its umbrella but we cannot try them all today and we still have an evening meal with wine to negotiate. It is a hard life.

Recently back home in England I was in one of the generic wine stores that we find on most retail parks and spotted a display securely housed behind the counter. On it were several bottles of de Ladoucette Pouilly Fumé. I asked to be able to go and have a look explaining that we knew the wine from our travels. I was somewhat surprised to find it here although to be fair we have used this store often and they have improved their stocks immensely over the years. There was no price on the display although from the neighbouring bottles I could discern it would be quite expensive. It was. At around twice the price of a fine bottle of Sancerre and about six times the price we paid for this bottle in France. I felt my wallet securing itself in my pocket. The assistant in the store was very persuasive but I could not justify the cost and contented myself with a promise to return to Sancerre and Pouilly to enjoy another visit and buy at the source.

This first wine tour is quite short and has given

us only a limited time to bond with our fellow wine loving travellers but we will embark on another tour a couple of years later that will take in much the same area but also Southern Burgundy. This will provide more education about the world of French wine but also some most interesting encounters with our fellow man. On our way home we had one final stop to make and for us it would be with the most famous of sparkling wines – Champagne.

# CHAMPAGNE

I am probably correct in saying that until this particular visit to France I had never tasted Champagne. In fact, the earlier visit to the Dampt brothers in Tonnerre had given me my first taste of sparkling wine in any form. I had certainly enjoyed that introduction and the prospect of a visit to a genuine Champagne house was an exciting prospect. On the journey going back north to Champagne I also sensed that this version of wine did bring out a certain snobbery in one or two of my fellow travellers. Famous names of Champagne houses such as Bollinger, Pommery, Mumm and Veuve Clicquot were bandied around as producers, giving the impression that they were on personal terms with the owners. I felt a little out of my depth as my Champagne knowledge and connections were non-existent. It was with very great relief that the coach drew up at the relatively modest house of Petit le Brun et Fils, 10 rue Lombard 51190, Avize. This is a small village set in beautiful rolling Champagne countryside just a short distance south of Epernay at the junction of the D40 and D19. This particular area of the Champagne region is designated as the Cotes de Blancs and consists of the villages of Cramant, Avize, Oger and Le Mesnil. The Champagne produced here is said to have character and not as soft or delicate as other areas. The well-known house of Pommery has a preference for this region and uses grapes from Oger. The family house of Le Brun is very French country style, a fine building that has great style but not too grand. I was extremely happy that we had not turned into one of the daunting Champagne houses that line the main thoroughfare in Epernay or Reims. This domaine was delightful and comfortable. It was on a scale that I felt appropriate to my limited knowledge of the product. I was however extremely willing to learn more.

The welcome as always is warm but slightly formal as befits the setting. The father and mother Le

Brun who own the domaine have their son to take charge of running the operation and the younger man will take us around the cellars. They are as we English would say 'well to do'. Champagne is clearly a prosperous business to be in and madam is dressed finely, expensive accompaniments complimenting her stylish outfit. Monsieur also clearly enjoys the fruits of his labours and he casts an observing eye over our party through his spectacles which he from time to time contemplatively allows to hang around his neck as he gets the measure of us. Monsieur Le Brun is undoubtedly a bon viveur and he reminds me in appearance and manner of that great English chef and lover of all things gastronomic Keith Floyd. His son is dressed as one would expect in a more casual manner as he is the one who takes charge of the physical side of the production. Everyone is a little diffident and standing back from them, unsure as to how to proceed until our tour and wine guide comes over and introductions are properly made and the ice is broken. From then on we all become a most lively and happy crowd.

The Le Brun family have produced Champagne under their own name since 1962 but the history of the house and vineyard go back nearly 300 years in time. The younger man guides us first of all on a tour of the cellars. This feels like a dangerous trip into the unknown and certainly it was for Niamh. Access to the cellars is by an old, ancient really, small industrial lift that takes only four people at a time. It has the appearance of a colliery lift ready to go down a mine shaft and I half expect that we will be issued with helmets and a candle or even a canary. This is not your fancy Champagne house in Reims. For Niamh this is a place to confront her worst fears. She hates lifts with a vengeance. As I look around the party I sense she is not alone and I scan the floor to see if anyone has passed out at the prospect of the terrors of descending below. Fortunately everyone does take their turn in this fearsome contraption and we are all safely gathered in the cellars deep below ground. The Le Brun cellars are around thirty metres below the village so this is a real test for anyone with a tendency towards claustrophobia.

These cellars are astonishing. They are hewn out of what appears to be pure chalk and they extend for miles underneath the village. Gallery after gallery of long arched tunnels stretch out in every direction. Cellars like these were genuine lifelines to many of the population of these wine producing regions during the Nazi occupation and you can only speculate that these at Le Brun also would have many tales to tell. During both world wars the people of the region used these deep cellars to avoid the bombing that particularly affected Reims. This meant that consequently casualties were relatively low compared to other towns and cities.

When one thinks of the grand Champagne houses you have to come to the conclusion that their production must be enormous to feed all the demand of customers and restaurants throughout the world. What has taken us aback here is that Petit Le Brun is a relatively small producer, away from the fashionable centres of Epernay and Reims. Yet even here every wall and crevice of these endless cellars is lined with row upon row of Champagne bottles. The numbers must run into the tens of thousands.

We are led down many of these passageways by the younger Le Brun and he makes comment on the sights before us which our guide translates.

Many bottles are led flat and stacked together, these are the bottles that have finished their fermentation. Many thousands of other bottles are housed in V shaped wooden frames called pupitres, similar to artists easels. The bottles are set into angled holes cut into the wood for that purpose. He explains the reason for the bottles being stored at an angle in these frames and also a process that makes you appreciate why Champagne is an expensive wine to buy and produce. He demonstrates the quarter turn of the bottle that is essential to be performed each day. Using both hands, with a quick flick of the wrists he is off on his mission. This is a process called remuage or riddling. To prevent a build-up of sediment in one place in the bottle and also to keep the fermentation active this arthritis inducing action must be done religiously each day. The angle of the bottle is gradually increased until by the end of the process the bottle is virtually upside down in the frame. He readily acknowledges that in later life all Champagne producers still following this traditional manual method of turning will indeed suffer the consequences of it. His prowess at this process is such that I can only fear that his wrists will not last him much more than a few more years as he rapidly turns the bottles on one side of the frame in around ten seconds before moving on down the line. A man (a remueur) who is highly skilled at this operation is said to be able to turn over 30,000 bottles a day. He will do this for around three months until the sediment is ready for the next step. I sincerely hope that his wife does not ask him on his return home if he had a nice day.

The cellars are very dry but cool and the conditions are perfect for the storage of these many thousands of precious bottles. With people from our party heading off in all directions under the village it is difficult to see how we will all find our way back to the surface. Thankfully nobody turns the lights out and we all eventually regroup at the foot of the ancient lift shaft. I imagine that if anyone did flick the light switch a considerable number of the party would have freaked out, especially as we all now have to face the ordeal of entering this rickety old lift to return to the surface. The more nervous of our party are taken up first and we all gather at the top of the shaft where there is a room containing an intriguing piece of equipment.

This device allows a two stage process that takes the bottle to the final corking and wire cage wrapping that we are familiar with as buyers.

Firstly, the neck of the Champagne bottle is submerged by the younger man into an extremely cold brine solution that freezes the portion of wine that is holding the sediment that has collected in the neck of the bottle during the riddling process. The bottle is then placed at an angle away from the body into a hooded container space. The crown cap is removed from the bottle with great care taken to ensure that only a minimum amount of the precious liquid is lost. The younger Le Brun does this in a conventional manner and the frozen wine holding the sediment in place is ejected at high velocity due to the dissolved $CO_2$ in a process that is called disgorgement.

The bottle is quickly topped up with a prescribed dosage of liqueur d'expedition. This is a mixture of a wine and sugar solution that will determine the sweetness of the finished Champagne, balance acidity, and assist in producing the desired flavour. The bottle is then corked and the traditional wire cage secures the cork in place. It is quite a dramatic process and of course has to be repeated for all of the bottles in that year's production.

If we found that demonstration dramatic then it was nothing compared with the skill displayed by the younger man's father. He took what can only be described as a small sword and proceeded to decapitate another bottle with this instrument and send the frozen sediment out of the bottle at the same high speed. Not a process to be tried with shaky hands but clearly he had performed this party trick many, many times and he executed it superbly. We were most impressed. He was obviously not yet ready to cede his crown to the younger man.

After all that excitement we were shown to a dining room that in décor was quite a step back in time. This was not Parisian shabby chic but more a room in keeping with the style of the late 19$^{th}$ century. The tables and chairs were of dark oak and in the corner stood an antique grandfather clock, alongside which on the long wall was a most unusual decorative piece, again in dark oak, looking very Germanic. Either side of this were two deer skulls with their full sets of antlers still attached. It felt more like a room where large glasses of foaming steins of beer would be brought out to the tables with sausages and sauerkraut. Instead we were going to be served fine Champagne and a lunch of regional cold meats and cheeses. It was all very convivial and the Le Brun family were very hospitable and madam despite her chic attention to her dress and grooming seemed most content to be acting as waitress to our party.

Of course there was a serious side to all this

and that was to persuade us to open our wallets and order some Champagne. We were extremely happy to do so. The prices of the Champagne were to our heavily taxed English minds unbelievably reasonable. Looking at them online today the prices have risen considerably and that to some degree is probably down to so many English visitors like us expressing astonishment that the price is so cheap. I have to say that even accounting for this inflation they are extremely good value for a high quality product. The Champagne produced here at Le Brun is mainly a blend of different years and this is common throughout Champagne as it enables a consistent, recognisable product to be obtained and be a trademark of the domaine. As is now the fashion among modern drinkers the Champagne will be mainly Brut (dry) although here they do offer a demi-sec version which will have around five percent of sugar added. Le Brun also in good years will offer vintage Champagne, one that is of that specific year only. We bought a couple of bottle of vintage Champagne that we had destined to be opened at our children's weddings. One has been used but our son's bottle is still unopened and I am now most unsure as to the quality of this now aged bottle of

Champagne.

The orders were fulfilled and a heavy pallet full of cases of Champagne was taken outside by a manual forklift. Everyone stood around silently watching as the young man pulled this pallet up a slope with his father pushing and guiding from behind. I could not help wondering why our coach driver did not bring the coach to the road at the bottom of the slope to save this backbreaking work but the load was eventually transferred and we bid fond farewells with a promise to return, which we kept.

# HEADING SOUTH

Our first real excursion into wine territory with only ourselves for company was when we drove south to Provence the year after our wine tour into the Loire valley. I recalled our stay close to Avignon in the village of Pujaut in my book THYME FOR PROVENCE. It was on this trip to Provence that we took our first steps of going out on our own with the confidence to explore and search out a wine degustation for ourselves. First of all we went into this head first by going the short distance from Pujaut to the world famous wine village of Châteauneuf du Pape.

In retrospect, Châteauneuf was not really the best or most advisable place to have begun but there we were. The village is very much a wine theme park and an upmarket one at that. The wines as you will appreciate are quite expensive and every other property contains an outlet for a producer, some more grand than others. It is a village where money congregates but the wines if chosen wisely are undeniably world class. It was difficult to know what to do, it has to be said we were quite intimidated by the expanse of choice on offer. We also felt that we did not as yet know very much about wines as good as this so did not wish to appear foolish and naïve. In the region as a whole there are many cooperatives that dispense the wine from a collection of growers. These outlets are not in the least intimidating and I hoped to find one here but Châteauneuf is not that sort of place. I felt so ill at ease that I initially drove through the village and out on the other side, stopping by a vineyard for contemplation. The cicadas were at full volume and the wide rows of vines stretching very beautifully into the distance. It was noticeable that the ground here was very stony and these stones are quite large. We were to learn that the reflective quality of these stones baked the grapes to some extent and consequently the wines here are distinctive and high in alcohol content. I felt calmer and we headed back to park our car in the village.

Châteauneuf is very much the preserve of the individual producer and they compete for your attention in a confident manner. My English reserve was in danger of holding me back. After walking back and forth through the narrow streets a number of times we turned again out of the small square at the heart of the village and came once more to Domaine La Boutinière Rue Commandant Lemaître, 84230 Châteauneuf-du-Pape. As we came to it, deliberately walking on the opposite pavement, I just could not avoid the gaze of the jolly man standing in the doorway who beckoned us to come inside for a tasting. In view of the prices of the wine it was with some trepidation that I felt obliged to take up his offer. Niamh and I were seated in sumptuous leather armchairs directly in front of our newly found wine tutor. If you had parachuted me into a village deep in the African jungle I could not have felt more out of place or uneasy. I had a lot to learn and a long way to go in my wine education and also in gaining personal confidence to deal with people who really knew their stuff but in this man we had a gentle touch from him and he quickly put us at ease.

What followed taught us a lot about the wines of the region in a very short space of time. In perfect English our friend explained about the *terroir* and there is no denying that these people are very possessive, protective of their special region. The wines are not to be called Cotes du Rhone which essentially is what they basically are, but you must call them distinctively the wine of the Popes – Châteauneuf du Pape. We would learn in the years to come as we travelled often to this region that exceptional red wines could be obtained at more modest prices but there is a certain cache about the name Châteauneuf. Our friend finally came to the end of his long speech and interesting and informative as it was I was desperate for a tasting. I have to be honest and say that I was also looking for a way out as I had finally seen the full price list on his desk – I can read upside down in French. So the tasting began and surprisingly the first wine was a white Châteauneuf du Pape - surprising because I was not aware that they made one. In mitigation of my ignorance it is quite a rare bottle, in fact the production of white wine from the appellation is limited to around only 5% of the total Châteauneuf output. It is also made up of a blend of grapes - 40% clairette, 30% grenache, 15%

bourboulenc, 15% roussane. It is a fine wine but one to be drunk with food, preferably fish or seafood. It is not one for enjoying as an aperitif or quaffing in the sunshine relaxing in the garden. It is quite full bodied and around 14% in alcohol strength. A good start and it is the cheapest bottle on offer so maybe I could get away with buying one of these and heading for the exit.

On to the main course – the reds.

Our host was very clever in how he presented his selection as he started the tasting with the cheapest bottle and worked his way up to the crème de la crème. The domaine only really produces two distinct Châteauneuf du Pape wines – Vieilles Vinges (100 year old vines) and the wine named after the Domaine - Le Domaine La Boutiniere and it was this wine he concentrated on. The price was based purely on the age and quality of the year in which the grapes were picked. This wine is again a blend - 70% grenache noire, 10% cinsault, 10% mourvèdre, 10% syrah. Some producers can use as many as a dozen grape varieties in a bottle of Châteauneuf. The difference between the various vintages was astonishing to our untrained palates. It was also clear that the better and older the vintage then the taste was that much more refined and deep. By the time we had reached the wine that he knew was going to impress us the most we had all but forgotten the cheapest bottle we had started with. The final wines really coated the glass and the fruit was deep in flavour. Even we novices could only splutter out superlatives at the gorgeous flavour and indeed the texture as it was so rich. He leant back in his chair, his face beaming with pride and satisfaction as he saw just how much we had been impressed by the taste and quality of his family's wines – years of tradition contained in a bottle. So, what are we to do? We know and he knows that there is no comparison between the first and last wines that he has dispensed to us. There is also no comparison in price. The top of the range bottle is pitched at a level that I would generally expect to pay to purchase a case of 12 wines from the Sunday Times Wine Club. Is it going to be an insult to him if we go for the cheaper version? He knows that we have to concede that it is at this moment in its young life a wine that is inferior by some considerable distance to the finest bottle. I cannot justify the price of the best, I just cannot. I am still feeling my way in learning and experiencing wine and not yet ready to make such an investment. So,

I go for a couple of bottles of the white and then a couple of the younger wines, assuring our teacher that I will keep them to mature and enjoy them when they have reached the age of his very finest bottle - the bottle that he saved until the end. He was happy but I feel sure that he felt that I was depriving myself of a life enhancing experience.

We eased ourselves from the soft skinned, incredibly comfortable armchairs, collected our small box of his wines and bid him goodbye with a promise to return. I still have one of his bottles maturing slowly back here in England. I still have not returned as there is so much to see and taste in France and also I just know that next time I really will have to pay the price and I am still not ready to do that.

A wine type we had become fond of and particularly enjoyed in the summer is rosé. I had carried out a little research on the subject and this was mainly using the English wine expert Oz Clarke's annual wine guide to help me along. With his expert advice I had come to decide that the villages of Lirac and Taval that are located close by our holiday home in this region just north of Avignon are ideal places to try and buy some rosé wines. It was indicated that these are villages that produce some of the most respected rosé wines in France. Rosé wine produced here is said to be longer lasting than most and consequently is higher in alcohol content than other softer rosé wines. We drove around the country lanes of the area for a while as it is a beautiful wine producing region and finally settled on quite a modest looking operation - Domaine Lafargue et Fils, 30126 Saint Laurent Des Arbres. This village is almost directly across the Rhone River from Châteauneuf du Pape and just north of the village of Lirac. Reflecting its modest outlook we had a short and rather perfunctory tasting but left with a couple of bottles of rosé to be enjoyed for lunch the next day. We drank a bottle with food but the effect on our constitution was unlike any other rosé that I had ever tried before and it soon became clear that we were not feeling that great and certainly not enjoying the usual feeling of wellbeing expected after a couple of glasses of rosé. I had not noticed the strength of the wine which was closer to a full bodied red that the lower level of rosé we would generally find in England. It was another lesson learnt – check the bottle first. It also educated us a little more as to what we really enjoy in a wine and sadly for us rosé of this strength was not enjoyable at all. There may have been absolutely nothing wrong with the bottle from a technical point of view but we did not enjoy it and at the end of the day wine is for pleasure and you must seek out the ones you really enjoy.

Before we moved on from the area there was one excursion that I wanted to make and it was to compare the wines of the Rhone just to the north of Châteauneuf to see how they compared in quality to the expensive wines we had tried in the village. We would only have time for a short trip and so we decided on a name that we were aware of – the village of Gigondas. When you arrive at wine villages like Gigondas the striking thing is that they are so small. They truly are little unspoilt villages despite the name being known throughout the world for the product bearing the name.

Gigondas is a village that consists mainly of a central square that houses the Mairie of course but also a fine gastronomic restaurant L'Oustalet, 5 Place Gabrielle Andeol, 84190 Gigondas. The overall effect of having such a lovely restaurant with the terrace spilling out into the square is very pleasing. A fine place for an artist to sit and paint in the shade of the trees. It is just the sort of village we envisioned finding in Southern France, it is the picture we carried with us in our imagination. Above the village there is an historic ruined Château that can be visited and this vantage point gives excellent views over the village to the Rhone plain. Looming behind that is the dramatic backdrop of the mountains – Dentelles de Montmirail. The chiselled ridge of these peaks, named it said because of the resemblance to fine lace structure, are visible all around this region and are a natural barrier to the plains beyond. Going around these hills gives a wonderful driving (or cycling) experience. We would in years to come be particularly fond of the route taking you up to the even smaller village of Suzette that offers views to the peak of Mount Ventoux. Today we would at the end of our visit to Gigondas make that journey for the first time. As you get near to Suzette there is a fine wine producer on the left coming from Beaumes de Venise – Château Redortier. It is well worth a visit to this domaine set in a unique location in the shadow of the Dentelles de Montmirail as they have an excellent reputation. The vineyards are at a relatively high altitude and are exposed to the full southern sun.

Close to the château in Gigondas you will find the village church – Saint Catherine d'Alexandrie.

No matter the size of the commune the churches in French villages will always be large enough to house at least three times the resident population. In the town around and just off the square there are a number of artisans, especially a first rate pottery – Artisans Potiers Element Terrre from whom we happily bought a couple of delightful pieces. There are a number of outlets in and around the village for some local wine producers and you could park in the village and happily walk to two or three for a degustation. Our destination of choice however is located just below the village.

 The producer we wanted to find was Domaine de Font-Sane 84190 Gigondas as after a little research this seemed a good all round quality grower. It was not easy to find but eventually a small sign indicated that we take a narrow road that leads on to an even smaller track and the pretty domaine is to be found surrounded by the stunning vineyards. The domaine is about 16 hectares (40 or so acres) divided into red and rosé Gigondas, red and rosé Ventoux. From the Domaine itself, you can get an even better view of the tiny village protected and dominated by the majestic rock faces of the Dentelles. The domaine name comes from the area "Fontsaine" which is situated high above the village where Domaine Font-Sane has terraced vines (restanques). Something we would discover on later visits was that some of the vineyards are extremely high up in the hills and sometimes quite exposed to the famous mistral blowing down the Rhone valley.

The tasting room here at Font-Sane is quite small but once again we are welcomed as old friends just as we are emerging from our car. The lady invites us inside and we see that glasses bearing the domaine logo are already set out for a tasting. We explain that although we had come to taste the reds on offer we noticed that they produce rosé wine also and she is happy to give up a sample of that first. It is lovely and fresh but the wine that was intriguing us is the red they produce. We tasted two versions of their red wines.

First was Gigondas Font-Sane Tradition, a blend of mainly grenache and syrah with a small amount of mourvèdre and cinsault. The vineyards that are cultivated have a soil of limestone and clay mixed with alluvium and loam but also containing many pebbles. The land is sandy and parched as you would expect in this sun baked region.

The second was Gigondas Font-Sane Terrasses

des Dentelles and one that the lady was especially proud to let us try. This is almost entirely made with grenache and syrah and the soil is limestone and clay based. Both wines are aged in oak and will keep for many years as my wine supply at home still gives testament to. I must I suppose finally open the last couple of bottles from this first visit but I need a special occasion or maybe a visit from the best of friends.

Both wines are an incredible colour, almost of garnets. They are richly fruity as if made exclusively from red berries, blackcurrants and blackberries rather than grapes. It is the spice that comes through that is so impressive and a feature of the wines of the south. If I have to be pushed on this I genuinely would say that I prefer these wines in the hills below the Dentelles to the exclusive and pricier wines of Châteauneuf. These wines here in Gigondas are superb and with red meat or cheese back home in the long English winter they are going to give great pleasure. They are quite complex wines really as they offer so much in characteristics but you certainly do not have to be a wine expert to enjoy them.

While we are having our tasting a young man, presumably the lady's son, comes into the room just in time to greet two visitors who seem to have an appointment. The smartly dressed lady and gentleman turn out to be representatives of a very famous Michelin starred restaurant in the centre of London. I will not give the name away but there is actually a clue in what I have just written. They are here to try the latest vintage that is now ready for storage in the restaurant cellars although the wines here can be drunk relatively young. Kept a few years they improve and no doubt will carry a heavy premium on the restaurant wine list. The young man takes them farther inside the domaine and we can no longer listen in to their conversation but it is an excellent indication that we have made an admirable choice in coming here.

A couple of cases are stowed away in the car and we are bid a cheery farewell but this thankfully will not be the only time we visit this producer and it is one of the best vineyard finds we have made on our journeys through France. We return in future years every time we are in the region.

One product that is inescapably linked to the region and just as treasured as the beautiful wines produced here is olive oil. We use a large amount in our cooking these days and wanted to take some genuine Provencal oil back home to England with us. On the other side of the Dentelles there are some large areas of olive groves and we had been told the journey over to the plain on the other side was spectacular - so it proved. The road from Beames de Venise winds up to the tiny village of Suzette and you pass along the way many cyclists, some using oxygen, looking forward to the downhill stretch on the other side. Once beyond Suzette the view stretches out in a never ending panorama with the dominating feature of Mont Ventoux looming in the distance. The road at Suzette splits into four directions and we took the Route de Suzette that winds slowly and carefully down the hillside to eventually find the village of Le Barroux. The drive is worth making for the landscape pleasures alone but we have a bonus at our destination that is set amongst the olive groves just outside the village – La Tuiliere, 84330 St Hippolyte le Graveyron. At a bend in the road just before you reach the D938 is a small track that you can take towards the olive growing estate. It goes on for quite some distance with lush productive olive trees either side of the driveway. It is a very fertile portion of land and extremely photogenic. Eventually you reach the domaine and your attention is immediately diverted by the sight of a vintage American Ford car in front of the property. It is an unexpected vehicle to see in such a setting but we investigate before we go up to the house. The car is in immaculate condition and bears American plates but I sense it rarely gets a run out in the country roads around Provence.

Our curious presence is spotted from the house and a friendly lady warmly welcomes us. She realises that we are English (not difficult) and is genuinely astonished that we want to taste and purchase some olive oil. She must have heard about our preponderance of 'chip' fat back in England - but we are not all savages. She happily shows us to the small tasting room but seems still most unsure that we actually know where we have come to and what we are going to taste. I reassure her that we really do love olive oil and we are interested in her product and in how they produce it. La Tuiliere is a family estate and the buildings date back to the $16^{th}$ century. She explains that they have well over a thousand olive trees under production and some are really old, going back over 500 years. She is generous with her information although all this is in French as she speaks not a word of English. They produce here at

La Tuiliere over 3000 litres of olive oil of different grades and to do that they require over 15000 kilos of olives. The clay soil holds any water available to the land and the limestone prevents it from becoming too wet. Also as in wine growing regions this warms the soil and reflects the sun. The olives at La Tuilerie she says are of a variety called 'verdale'. This type stays green even when they are fully ripe and is resistant to frost. This is important as the winters here can be extremely cold, something you tend not to realise about Provence. Two harvests are generally made, one in November that produces an oil with a distinctive taste that should not be used until after the following July. Secondly, she also says that they harvest other trees up to the end of December when the olives have become very ripe and this is soft, delicate oil that should be used early and before July. They also pick the olives by raking by hand, a very laborious and labour intensive method but the tradition is clearly important to them.

The production is also traditional. The olives are taken to a press in the nearby village of Caromb and are washed and crushed. The mixture produced of oil and water is separated by centrifugal force and the oil is placed in stainless steel tanks. This first cold pressing gives the finest quality extra virgin olive oil for use in dressings, marinades and in cooking. Other pressings will produce lighter oil suitable for basic cooking.

We taste three different types of oil and settle on the one we want to buy and look forward to using in England. The lady draws off the oil from a tank and we are happy to pay what to us is a quite expensive sum for a five litre container of this wonderful oil. It is a place where quality supersedes quantity and the price although much higher than we would pay for a Greek or Spanish extra virgin oil in a supermarket back home seems more than reasonable when you understand the care and love going into the production. Even at the end of our encounter our host is still a little bemused that we English actually want to buy her oil and are being sent away as happy customers. We reassure her that we will not be coming back for a refund but that it really has been a joy to visit her domaine. We will return in future as once you have tried oil from a source like this and appreciate that it cannot be bettered, you will be spoilt as to having to use an alternative supermarket brand when it inevitably runs out.

We moved on after a couple of days to the village of Lourmarin which is a small commune in the Southern Luberon in the Provence-Alpes-Côte d'Azur region to the south and east of Avignon. Again the story of my encounter with our crazy host Bernadette at the villa in the town I have recounted in my book THYME FOR PROVENCE. I will not go over that again, it is still ingrained on my memory but it will make you smile and is well worth reading.

It was from this base that we visited a domaine that I had learnt about a few years previously when I watched the food and wine programmes involving Rick Stein and in this case Keith Floyd. I spoke about Val Joanis in my Provence book but it is essential that I refer to it in this book on wine touring as Val Joanis is key to our wine education and a spur to encouraging us to explore France much more fully. The Château Val Joanis, Pertuis 84120 winery and gardens are located off the D973 heading west from Pertuis and not to missed if you are in the area and by that I actually mean if you are in France. It is worth a visit for the beautiful terraced gardens that are filled with everything that is seasonal in flowers, plants, fruit and vegetables creating an oasis of self-sufficiency, protected from the Mistral wind, the wind that sends artists mad.

Floyd filmed here on a wine tour of France that he undertook for the BBC and true to form he enjoyed plenty of tastings. It was his enthusiasm for Val Joanis that inspired me, on a day that he filmed in searing heat, tasting the domaine reds at far too high a temperature and pushing himself and his able companion close to collapse. It was great TV but not ideal for getting the best out of the wines but he left such an impression on me with his boyish enthusiasm that coming here was an essential part of our tour to the sun baked south.

The gardens are a joy, but just watch out for the enormous hornets that feast on the lavender. I am not a fan of wasps at the best of times but can cope with the odd bee or two. However, these monsters were the stuff of science fiction and I gave them a very wide berth although fortunately they do seem to congregate rather than make any attempt to follow and intimidate you. The terraces lead to open views of the countryside and for any gardener these paths and beds are a real delight, fruit and vegetables mixed in with the most stunning displays of flowers and shrubs with lavender of course taking centre stage. The added bonus is that some of the produce is made available to the visitor and what could be more perfect than fresh fruit and vegetables prepared simply and eaten in the Provencal sun with a glass of the estates rosé wine. It is very pleasant to stroll around the gardens prior to a tasting and also if the winery is busy it is a perfect place to await your turn.

Val Joanis wines as you would expect reflect the *terroir* of this sun drenched region but perhaps more than anything else they contain the sunshine that beats down on the exposed vineyards around the château. It is through the vineyards and olive groves that you drive to reach the domaine, a site originally of a Roman villa. The buildings and gardens are quite some distance from the main road. On our first couple of visits here the long drive was rather rough and rocky and really a four wheel drive vehicle would have been a more suitable companion but we got there eventually. The driveway is now smooth and well maintained so no further worries on that score.

We have had many enjoyable tastings here at Val Joanis but the first one inspired by Floyd's exuberance was another part of our introduction to French wines and the variety that the country is capable of producing. This visit was extremely informative as it was conducted by one of the owners and producers at the domaine. We were taken through the range on offer from the two white wines - Cuvée Les Aubépines and the Château Val Joanis Blanc Tradition through their rosé wines on to the splendid reds of Rouge Tradition and Cuvée Les Griottes. As lovely as the white and rosé wines are it was for the reds that we had come on this first visit although in years to come we would appreciate the white and rosé much more. One of the joys of touring France and visiting the vineyards is that you can share your experiences in the form of a bottle or two with friends at your dining table and this we happily began to do. Sharing a bottle of Val Joanis becomes a regular feature in our lives. Our friends always looked forward to our return from France with the boot of our car fully laden – it took 96 bottles to fill it and there was always the back seat. Val Joanis Cuvée Les Griottes Rouge became our 'house red'. In all the years since these first visits and the hundreds of bottles we have brought back from visiting the vineyards of France it is this red that our house guests have consistently voted to be the very finest bottle we have found. It is a blend of syrah and grenache grapes grown on vines that are rooted in rocky, pebbly soil, matured for around 10 months in barrels. The wine is exceptionally fruity, not too heavy, a wine than can be enjoyed without food although it is at its best when poured at the dining table. It is a standout example of the winemaker's art; full of the Provencal sunshine and of course that indefinable *'terroir'*. It is obtainable in the UK but it is a special thing to be able to taste and purchase on site at this ancient bastide, one of our very favourite wine locations in France and we return for fresh supplies as often as we are able.

Starting back from the village of Lourmarin it is a pleasant though hilly and winding drive along the D943 between tall rocky outcrops that eventually lead you to a view of the Luberon and the numerous villages perched on the hills, the first of which is Bonnieux. This village is our favourite in the Luberon with plenty of character amongst its ancient streets, great food in restaurants such as Le Fournil and spectacular views over the Luberon countryside. It is less busy and touristy than many of the other famous villages such as Gordes, Roussillon and Menerbes, the village made famous by Peter Mayle in 'A Year in Provence'.

It is on the outskirts of the village that our view

of French wines took another unexpected turn – we discovered the joy of the French wine cooperative. Here on the plain below Bonnieux is La Cave de Bonnieux, a one hundred year old enterprise that gathers the best that the growers on this fertile land have to offer. The prices here were astonishing and in line with what we had found in the Languedoc on that first visit to France. The range of course is complete - red, white, rosé and 'méthode traditionnelle brut' – white or rosé fizz. They dispense the wines also by the petrol pump type method and you can fill your container with extremely good wine at giveaway prices. They also now sell in boxes of 5 or 10 litres. This however is not just a place to go in and pick up a relatively cheap bottle that you know nothing about and take a chance that you will enjoy it. No, they have a fully set up tasting area and will happily guide you through the range on offer and you are sure to find something to suit your palate and most certainly your wallet. This is a place to set up your stay in a gite, always to have a selection on offer for your stay but also these wines are so good that it is worth taking a selection back home with you – they travel very well.

The area is full of small domaines that offer a

degustation and in future years we would seek these out and often just call in at one we were passing by and be warmly welcomed for a degustation. If you are starting off in searching out and trying French wine as we were at this time then these cooperatives are a fine place to make a start. They are all over France and even in Burgundy you will find them. Especially in a more up market and bewildering region such as Burgundy they are probably the best place to begin.

Our first visit to Provence was fairly tentative – baby wine steps really but we had made the effort to try to learn by visiting some domaines. We had not done a lot but we were learning and more than that we were enjoying ourselves immensely. Not only that but our friends back home were becoming even better friends every time we returned – just kidding. It was in truth though a means to get to know some acquaintances much better when finding we had a shared interest in wine and food and many special friendships have blossomed with our new found interest. One thing I was determined not to allow to happen was that I became a wine snob, someone for whom the bottle becomes more important than the contents. I would always concentrate on finding less well known producers who were turning out exceptional wines mainly under the radar and providing incredible value. To do this I needed more confidence to drive up to a wine cave door and this would come after going on another organized wine tour. Before we did that we took the car over the channel to Normandy and headed south to the Western Loire to stay at Chenonceaux, the village famous for its breath-taking château. From here we could explore the area and find a producer or two and it was now that we really started to have a preference for white wine, a love that had started in Sancerre the previous year.

# CHENONCEAUX AND TOURAINE WINES

It was November time when we arrived in Chenonceaux and the autumn air was cold and crisp with damp leaves on the floor and a mist obscuring the view to the top of the main street Rue du Docteur Bretonneau. The welcome at the Hotel Roséraie was by contrast very warm in all senses of the word and we were soon settled in a large room with what seemed an even more expansive bathroom. It was not five star by any means but it had character. The food served during our stay was local produce cooked simply and well and the restaurant had many reminders of Churchill, Truman, Eisenhower and the Americans passing through after D-Day. Like all of Normandy and the Loire Valley it is impossible to escape the relatively recent events that played out in the countryside, villages and towns of this region. Our history journey through these areas is for another book as it is a moving region to visit.

For now our focus before our wine gathering is that rather large house at the end of the hotel garden - Château de Chenonceau. Many places can be called magical and I am as guilty as anyone else of overusing that word but for Chenonceaux there really is no other English word to describe it. The expansive view is stunning as you approach the château through the formal gardens that were laid out over many centuries and maintained in the same original classical style. There is more to come and it the view from the side of the château looking over the still water that is the magical one. It is a view that is the most famous from a photographer's perspective and one of the most constantly depicted aspects in France. On a clear bright day such as this the reflection of the château in the tranquil water is despite the number of times it has been photographed a photo opportunity not to be missed. There is so much to see outside that you can linger for quite some time before actually going into the château itself. The gardens, although very formal and not especially to an English taste in some ways, are beautiful and immaculately maintained. There is a vegetable and produce garden that is full to bursting with good things, ready to be carried to the kitchen of the on-site restaurant that serves a cut above your usual tourist fare. The ever changing views of the château as you wander around the grounds force you to constantly stand and admire and photograph the scene. The fear though is that you will be disappointed with the château itself as many of the Loire châteaux such as Chambord are relatively sparse inside, their contents long since removed, especially around the time of the French Revolution. Chenonceaux happily escaped that fate by a quirk of circumstance and retained its character and contents and what treasures await the visitor inside.

The interior is sumptuous by any standards and the artworks and sculptures by the great masters such as Rubens and Van Dyck ensure that a visit here takes time and progress around the chateau will be slow, a new masterpiece takes your attention at every turn. The furniture is grand and extensive;

it has always been a home but on a scale that is magnificent in its splendour. There is one particular room that sums up the opulence and grandeur of the occupants and where their loyalties lay. This room has the most spectacular white fireplace, embellished in gold relief with two crowns standing proud. Next to this dominant structure is a large painting of the King –' Le Roi'. It is mounted in the most over the top gilded frame you will ever see – it screams out 'C'est moi – Le Roi'. It emphasises exactly where the occupant's loyalties were placed and who they depended on for their opulent lifestyle.

Walking around the château there are so many opportunities to be a little 'arty' with your photography, especially by using the black and white chequered flooring to draw the eye into a photo – it is a splendid place to visit and to take in the interest it provides at every turn. Thank goodness for digital photography but for our visit I had the restriction of 35mm film and I had to be more careful and particular when framing a shot.

Although we had not specifically come to the Loire for a wine excursion it was an ideal opportunity for us to find new wines and also to try out some of our new found knowledge and confidence in visiting individual domaines on our own. We had recently tried a Vouvray wine back in the UK and so for our first foray into this new region it was to that town we headed.

I had done a little research before we had left the UK so for our first visit I had settled on the Domaine Huet in the village of Vouvray - 11 rue de la Croix Buisée, 37210 Vouvray. The Domaine of Huet was founded in 1928 and is arguably the most familiar name to visitors in search of the distinctive wines of Vouvray, many of which are sweet or semi-dry although a dry (sec) version is also produced. Perhaps as much as any other wine region in France the wine makers of Vouvray and its environs place great emphasis on the type of soil that is available to them – the *'terroir'*. They actually describe their land, the *terre,* as sacred and you will always get the impression from the producers that France and its land, their land, is indeed blessed by God. Our visit to Huet would be one that left mixed feelings; the wines were superb but the experience left us disappointed for the first time really on our travels seeking out wine in France.

Domaine Huet produce four main varieties from the vines at their disposal – dry or sec, demi-sec or part dry, moelleux or sweet and pétillant, a sparking variety. One problem as a visitor and especially one coming to Vouvray for the first time is that this can be quite confusing as not all producers label the wines with simple defined distinctions between the types. You really do have to try them as it is quite easy to purchase or order a bottle in a restaurant and end up with something totally unsuitable for your meal. This is a more difficult village in which to make a purchase and in its own way as confusing as Burgundy, but more of that later. All the Huet wines are of the highest quality and many are bottles that can and do age well for several decades. They have three distinctive sites – le Haut-Lieu, Clos de Bourg and le Mont. In addition to the wines mentioned above they will extend themselves in the most exceptional years to producing a special vintage called Cuvee Constance which is a blend of the produce from all the parcels of land. There are no surprises about their production, this is traditional Vouvray and now also has a bio-dynamic aspect to the production that shows the differences between the parcels of land very clearly. We were impressed with the quality of these wines; they were at the top end of anything we had so far come across on our travels. However you sensed that they knew that and because of that attitude the host at this tasting fell well short in our expectations. For want of a better expression we felt that he was 'looking down his nose at us'. Granted we were still novices and did not know as much as we would have liked, though we were dressed well enough and had combed our hair, but we were left with the distinct impression than we should be buying on-line or in a supermarket, which was a shame.  We bought anyway, the wines won out and were enjoyed greatly back in England but I could not leave the Vouvray experience there – I had to find a friendlier producer and get the welcome we usually found at the welcoming sign of a degustation.

We found it a short distance away at Bernard Fouquet, Domaine des Aubuisieres 32 Rue Gambetta, 37210 Vouvray. The welcome was such a contrast to the one received at the earlier visit and the wines were exceptional and varied but again took a little more consideration to be able to understand the labels and the types we were going to taste. The visit here reemphasised the unique nature of the soil and vines in this particular small region, a micro climate of viniculture. The grapes used for Vouvray are chenin and as the years have passed I have to say that chenin blanc is probably to my palate one of the least favourite of wines, especially the examples from South Africa. The wine produced here in Vouvray bears no relation to the general production around the world from chenin and really that is the beauty of making the effort to travel around France in this way. You are going to find real gems in the vineyards and cellars of France and small villages like Vouvray can produce something unexpected and give great pleasure. Here M.Fouquet did that with the wines and this time also with a generous, warm welcome.

We settled on three wines to purchase after a full run through of his range of wines on offer. The first of these, Cuvee de Silex, specifically refers to the type of soil the chenin grapes have been grown in. Silex soil is a finely ground silica stone and just as around Chablis the soil is more a rocky structure than what we would usually know as soil in the UK. The 'Silex' wine is not totally sweet but does have this distinctive mineral taste which is also reminiscent of Chablis or Sancerre.

Cuvee Alexander is a still but very sweet wine and will keep for many years. In fact you can still buy versions of this from the domaine that are around 20 years old. What is amazing considering how long you can store some of these wines is that they are not actually very high in alcohol which you would expect if you were going to keep a Burgundy or Bordeaux. Another sweet wine that we brought back with us was 'Le Marigny' which again was relatively low in alcohol. Another still and fairly sweet wine we enjoyed was 'Le Plan de Jean' and as the name suggest is from a specific parcel of land and again distinctive, being very redolent of fresh fruity grapes. Finally of course it was a sparking version – Domaine des Aubuisieres Brut, as fine as any Champagne sold at twice the price of this example of gorgeous fizz. When well produced however it retains a character of its *terroir* rather than just trying to imitate the wines of the Champagne region. Sparkling wine from Vouvray is in much demand and around half of the total production from the region goes into making it.

What a joy this visit was, still memorable nearly 20 years down the line and to have such quality of wines discovered at source to enjoy back in the English winter is something you cannot put a price on.

Vouvray is the most well-known name to a

visitor from the UK or America but there is another beautiful wine produced just across the river at Montlouis. It is fine wine that is produced under the shadow of its more famous neighbour but well worth seeking out.

As I mentioned earlier one of the pleasures we have in life is to be able to share the wines we find on our French travels with our friends back home but on this occasion it came with an unexpected and slightly disturbing caveat. One essential thing to be aware of about wines from Vouvray and similar areas that produce a sweet wine is that some of the production comes from grapes that are left on the vine until they have almost rotted – botrytis or noble rot. This special wine is generally produced in larger quantities in years of the hottest summers. This beneficial bacteria and condensing of the grapes until they are quite shrivelled produces some distinctive wines. These extraordinary sweet wines can age for many decades and improve with the passing of time. What I was not aware of is that for some people it can inspire an allergy that can take quite a nasty turn and so it proved on the first time we served a sweet Vouvray wine at our table. One of our friends proved to be very allergic to this wine and the bacterial content and came out in a total body rash, finding it difficult to catch her breath with the added effect of raising a high body temperature in her. The symptoms lasted for well over an hour but did gradually wear off but it was more than a little scary encountering such a reaction to the wine. We took a great deal of care in making sure that she was steered well clear of this particularly concentrated and rotted Vouvray in the future.

One place that you must visit purely because of its dramatic situation on the river is the town of Amboise. The town is dominated by the Château d'Amboise that is atop a high cliff looking down over the Loire river. The château is famous because of a renowned visitor, one Leonardo da Vinci who came armed with some of his work to introduce Italian art to France. The aging Leonardo was invited to come to Amboise by the French king Francois I. Leonardo died here in Amboise and in the church of the grand château you will find this remarkable man's grave. His legacy can be seen in the architecture not just in this region but throughout France. Interestingly his most famous work, in fact the world's most famous painting, the Mona Lisa, was brought by Leonardo to France rather than being given to the man who commissioned the work. It entered into the collection of Francois I after Leonardo's death. The Mona Lisa also spend the period of the second world war in the region, being housed in châteaux of the area as were most of the paintings of the Louvre. The great survivor is of course back in the Louvre and has never returned permanently to Italy despite one brief visit when it was stolen from the museum.

After our stay in Chenonceaux we planned to head east and visit Sancerre once more but along the way there were a couple of producers of AOC Touraine sauvignon white wine that we wanted to visit. Touraine white is a very acceptable alternative to the more expensive Sancerre. For around half the price you can have a bottle that compares extremely well with its more illustrious neighbour. The same applies in Chablis where the village of St Bris produces a very fine alternative as I recall in this book. The first producer of Touraine was near to the commune of Saint Aignan driving east on the N76 - Domaine Bernard Ardois, 1063, route de Beauval, Roche 41110, SEIGY.

Finding the illusive M. Ardois was easier said than

done. We headed out of Saint Aignan towards the area where we thought the small hamlet of Seigny was located but found ourselves eventually staring at the large gates of the Zoo Parc de Beauval or Beauval Zoo as we found it was referred to locally. This was a little unexpected find to say the least in rural France but the unmistakable sight of non-local animals was there in front of our eyes. Not wishing to have my windscreen wipers interfered with I edged away from the entrance and worked my way back towards Saint Aignan by another route. There on the way was the domaine of Bernard Ardois, the vineyards located on an elevated position above the house and cellar. I could see work going on in the fields and we parked in the small courtyard of the house and rang the bell at the cellar door. The door was open but there seemed to be no one around and I rang again but to no avail. Going back outside I again saw someone in the fields above so we made our way around the winding path up to the vineyard hoping to attract his attention, although why I thought he might be able to break off from his important task in hand I am not really sure. As we approached the gate to the field the man was out of our view but suddenly a large dog appeared on the horizon moving at speed towards the gate, clearly endowed with a very angry disposition. Not one to fail to take a hint I encouraged Niamh to keep up the fast pace I had generated from a standing start back down the path to the security of the car. Arriving safely back at our vehicle I noticed that there was no sign of the chasing canine but there was a man in the distant field waving furiously at us, no doubt as angry as his dog about our straying onto the sacred '*terroir*'. Not so, as we soon realised he wanted us to stay by the cellar door as he was going to come down and greet us. He had clearly explained to his dog that we just wanted a degustation.

M. Ardois was full of apologies and was mortified that he may have potentially missed a visitor to the domaine. He checked that the bell was indeed working as his wife should have been around but I would leave them to sort out the domestic arrangements after we had gone. He was so friendly and welcoming and eager to open a few bottles to display his talents in producing Touraine wine from his part of this fertile region. The wines were so good and in a blind tasting I feel sure that you would have been led to feel that you could actually have tasted Sancerre. Perhaps the finish is not quite as long but the aroma and bouquet in the month is intense and very redolent of the mineral quality of the land. A pity it was not a warm summers day so to have got the full effect. Even on a very cool November day you could imagine the pleasure of quaffing this lovely wine back in the occasional hot summers day in England. The final wine would bring an unexpected and very pleasant consequence in a couple of years' time. This was his fizz - 'Touraine Méthode Traditionnelle Blanche'. A wine so comparable to Champagne that only the most fastidious lover of the finest Champagne houses would quibble at being served a glass. Back home after a very brief family conference over a tasting of this gorgeous sparkling wine it was unanimously decided that this would be the fizz to be served at our daughter Charlotte's wedding in the following year. Of course that meant the hardship of a return to Bernard Ardois and the Loire Valley and no doubt a revisit to Sancerre but I felt we could cope with doing that. We did just that and purchased a few cases and as expected we wowed all the guests with this exceptional wine and it added that 'sparkle' to a day of great joy.

On this first occasion we filled the boot of the car with incredible bargains to be enjoyed back home and M. Ardois furnished a couple of free gifts including a wine saver with the Domaine logo stamped on it. A thoughtful touch but I have to say I have never understood the concept of leaving any contents in a bottle.

Our next port of call was to be Domaine des Chézelles 18 rue du Grand Mont, 41140 Noyers-sur-Cher, an address I believe I picked up from an article in a Sunday newspaper supplement by Matthew Jukes who extoled the virtues of the wines of Alain Marcadet. Noyers is just a stone's throw away from Saint Aignan on the D976 and we soon found the domaine. Being so close to our previous visit we assumed the wines would be pretty much the same. Not so, for as we were learning, the beauty of visiting various domaines yourself and trying the wines is that you do start to understand the French word *terroir* more and more. Wine quality and taste vary from not only village to village but from field to field and that was evident here. Looking back over to Saint Aignan you could almost see the domaine of M. Ardois but the wines that M. Marcadet produces are not the same. The quality is just as high but the wines have a slightly less mineral quality and a little crisper, perhaps even more reminiscent of

Sancerre. We had found yet another very affordable gem in this region alongside the River Loire. Again the welcome is warm and generous with an apparent intention to let you sample all the wines but as I was driving and not a great spitter of fine wine we contented ourselves with just three and were very happy to add to the collection destined for England.

The region of the Loire valley to Sancerre and over to Chablis is an area that we had fallen in love with. Now we were gathering a wealth of knowledge about the wines, giving us much more confidence in approaching producers and seeing what was on offer in the various domaines in the region. It had to be acknowledged though that we were still novices, we felt that we could come to the Loire and search out new wines and to a lesser extent have confidence in travelling to Provence or the Languedoc. But one region terrified us – Burgundy. It was a region that we could not avoid if we wanted to explore the wines of France and nor did we want to. I felt that we needed some initial pointers; a guide that would help us avoid what I knew would be some inevitable pitfalls if we just dived in ourselves. Another wine tour came up and this not only gave us a chance to get more information on the area around

Chablis but would give us a fine introduction to Burgundy in the company of a Master of Wine. So, that was our next wine visit to France and it would set up our visits for years to come and inspire in us the confidence to make some memorable visits to so many extraordinary producers under our own steam.

# BURGUNDY – THE ANGELS SHARE

Our stay in Beaune as the centre point of our introduction to Burgundy was at the Hôtel Henry II Rue du Faubourg Saint-Nicolas, 21200 Beaune and a fine place to stay it proved to be. Beaune centre was a short stroll away and this would become a town that not only would we become very familiar with but immediately it would become a favourite ville in France. Once settled in the hotel we struck out on our own to explore the ancient streets of the wine town but never as yet finding the confidence to go into the many wine shops filled with the wines of the region. Especially intriguing are the bottles originating from the Hospices de Beaune with their hefty price tags – we still had a great deal to learn and we needed assistance. The ancient town of Beaune is the hub of the wine trade of Burgundy. Beaune as an appellation is an excellent one in its own right but of course is surrounded by many very famous village and commune names. Beaune is a beautiful town, full of attractive and interesting architecture and you need to explore inside the ancient walls of the town. Take time to walk along the many cobbled side streets, taking slim entrance ways to seek out the numerous fascinating narrow passageways before concentrating on the main event in the centre of the town – L'Hôtel Dieu.

This charitable hospital was founded in 1443 by Nicolas Rolin, chancellor of Philippe le Bon. Rolin is a name you will still see associated with winemaking in the Côte d'Or vineyards. This building is of high gothic architecture, it reflects the strong bond between Burgundy and Flanders. Its multi coloured polychrome roofs along with the golden colours of the Last Judgement alter piece by Rogier Van der Weyden have made this standout building famous. This medieval hospital also contains a multitude of other treasures including the great "Salle des Pôvres" with its highly sculpted and decorated ceiling, a gothic chapel, the pharmacy housing a collection of pewter and earthenware, the kitchen boasting an automated rotisserie. The Hospices de Beaune charity wine auction has taken place annually here at the Hôtel since 1859, and falls on the third Sunday in November as part of a three-day festival purely devoted to the food and wines of Burgundy - a festival known as Les Trois Glorieuses. The parcels of land relating to the hospital itself are owned as a non-profit venture and the wine auction can set high prices that go to charity but also become the benchmark guide as to the prices expected for that particular year's vintage. The three days are a joyous but highly prestigious occasion and to partake in the bidding would not be for the fainthearted. We would be wined and dined in Beaune on these next few days and also on other occasions in the future when we revisit but although I have been inside the Hospital I have not as yet had a table at the November festivities.

Around the hospital are many fine wine retailers and the bottles in the window displays are a who's who of famous names. One unusual one is the label on a bottle from a piece of land on one of the best vineyards, that of Grèves. A small parcel of that land is called L'Enfant Jesus and you will see bottles of that name in the shops. This rather colourful name came from the early wine producing monks and apparently it is derived from the expression that the wine 'goes down like little Jesus in velvet trousers'. I can only assume that was thought up after one too many late night drinking sessions in the local taverns or the crypt in the abbey.

On this visit our party group would be an eclectic one and we were to enjoy some interesting and stimulating company for the most part, but there were other parts also, believe me.

There were an older couple called John and Sylvia who were stimulating company. They have an equally interesting son who is familiar as a resident expert on the Antiques Roadshow on the BBC.

Jack and Hilary were from California and had made the long trip over to France especially to be on this tour. He was the epitome of a Silicon Valley executive and she a lady of many charitable causes but they were easy company and Jack did not talk about computers once on the trip.

There was Roger who was undoubtedly a man

that engaged in espionage in a former life, such a John le Carre character, a loner who must have had tales to tell but they remained discreetly hidden. The few words he offered were always interesting although they would never lead to a conversation but he savoured his wine with a knowledgeable air of contentment.

Henry was also a loner, very public school, highly educated but with an undeveloped personality that made it painful for him to engage with people. So you wondered why he had put himself through this ordeal of a socialising group experience. He was a harmless, good natured soul, extremely polite and impeccably mannered. He latched on to me from the start and was always by my side but I didn't mind as it eased him into the tour and he loosened up a little as time went on. He did love his wine and if you could prise it out of him had an extensive knowledge of French wines, far ahead of my limited scope.

Frank and Angela were elderly, in fact in their mid to late 80's - a more mismatched couple it would be hard to find. I felt so sad watching this pair who had been together for so long and even at this late stage of their lives were in total torment at being bound together. Well, that is not quite true as it was Frank that was in torment. I have rarely seen a man so mentally battered and beaten by this most obnoxious of women. She was oblivious to him as she did whatever she required without any consideration for him. He meekly accepted his non-role in the relationship and took the abuse, as it has to be said did the tour guide. The poor man also latched onto me to a degree if she was not around. He thoroughly enjoyed one day of touring when his wife stayed behind, for which he and everyone else was truly thankful. His joy that day seemed to say it was the happiest of his life which was dreadfully sad to think he had probably hated the previous fifty or sixty years.

Then there was Emma and Richard and they were so memorable that I have given them a chapter to themselves later on in the book, I promise I will not refer to them again in this chapter but they were shall we say – special.

There were of course many others but most kept a discreet distance with only brief interaction, it was never going to be party time for most but in the main it was a friendly collection of people that in a lot of ways had only a love of wine in common. Barriers were constantly broken down as the tour progressed although my Northern accent prevented full interaction on many occasions.

Here also were two people on the tour who stood out from the rest of the party as they were clearly not as concerned about the tastings but more focused on the technical aspects of the production and the viniculture. They were also the only people on the tour that we had encountered previously and that meeting was only a few weeks earlier. On a visit to Cornwall just prior to the tour we had paid a visit to - Camel Valley Vineyards, Nanstallon, Bodmin, Cornwall, PL30 5LG. We had heard about this English vineyard (Oh, and nobody laughs anymore when you say that) from a feature on television by Rick Stein. Rick was a friend and supporter of this vineyard which is located close to his empire in Padstow. The tasting and welcome we received was a real unexpected pleasure. The wines and especially the Champagne style sparkling wines including a gorgeous rosé were as fine as any we would taste in France. The vineyards are on a gently sloping hillside, very reminiscent of France. A perfect location to attempt what most people thought impossible –

produce quality wine in cold, wet England. We were more than happy to purchase a couple of cases and it was not just in sympathy to try to support an English venture. These wines were genuinely superb and could hold their own in any blind tasting, which in fact we did around our dining table with some knowledgeable friends – Camel Valley won that night.

As we were leaving the Cornish vineyard, carrying a couple of cases and walking back to our car, a man drove away from the house in an open topped sports car and gave a cheery wave to us both. This was the owner, Bob Lindo, an ex-RAF pilot whose career came to a dramatic end when he was seriously injured ejecting from a mid-air collision close to Helmsley in North Yorkshire, the recovery from which he modestly downplays. Bob started the Camel Valley vineyard about three years later with his wife Annie and the success of this venture is taken forward by his son Sam and the awards have continued to flow – even from the French.

On the ferry over to France at the start of the tour I was in the same queue for a cup of tea as Bob. I said to Niamh that I knew this man, perhaps I had come across him in my career, maybe someone in

IT that I had used in the past. It was not until we had got well into France that I realised who he was and in fact we had only 'met' him very recently. At the autoroute services he and his wife Annie were walking around outside and I intercepted them and said that I knew who he was. After explaining how we saw each other in Cornwall he remembered the day we had visited. He was also I think a little taken aback that he had been recognised as I believe that he would rather have remained incognito as a man on a mission to spy on the French. Later, on the coach the wine guide announced that we had a couple of famous wine makers on the tour and his occupation was well and truly out in the open but I can assure him that it was not me that informed the party in any way, I appreciated what he was trying to achieve on this visit.

Bob, on each domaine visit would ask quite technical questions and was always, as was Annie, keenly interested in walking into the vineyards and examining the soil, the *terroir*, learning all the time something new to put into practice if possible in English conditions. I recall one particular occasion when Bob had asked a producer something that no layman could possibly have needed to know and was met with total silence. French secrets were for the French and years of tradition and expertise were not going to be proffered easily to the cunning English. Time for a tasting as he quickly moved on, ignoring the question. Bob and Annie were an incredibly interesting couple as well as being the most delightful company although obviously Bob was lost in his own thoughts at times as he pondered on something he had seen or discovered. The vineyard back at Camel Valley has gone from strength to strength as we have seen when returning many times over the years. Surely something of the French know how has seeped back into the English *terroir* from his visit to Burgundy.

The Cote D'or is the most stunning of landscapes, gently sloping rolling countryside that leads up from the plain that heads south. Miles upon miles of fertile vineyards stretch up these slopes and the higher they go, the closer to the sun, the more these parcels of land are valued and the price of the finished bottle reflects its location of birth. It is also a region that for the novice is extremely difficult to understand and purchase wine with confidence. The appellations here are fixed in time and no one is going to allow a change to the way things are done here, tradition and *terroir* are paramount and that includes the labelling of the bottles. Back home we are now so used to a bottle in the supermarket being labelled – chardonnay, sauvignon blanc, merlot etc… that to arrive here and be confronted by bottles that only have the name of the village and possibly the grower or négociant is to say the least very confusing. To observe the array of bottles in a shop, sorry boutique, window with some carrying astonishing prices makes any purchasing decision a leap of faith. The first visit today puts us right in the centre of that minefield, to a producer that is right at the top end of quality and one that does not need to advertise, in fact there is not even a sign outside the door.

In the small but internationally famous wine village of Gevrey-Chambertin we are guided discreetly along the narrow streets to an unprepossessing house and taken to a side door. I sense that really we should have been blindfolded as well but an exception has been made for les Anglais. We have arrived at – Domaine Boillot Lucien & Fils, 1 Rue Docteur Pujo, 21220 Gevrey-Chambertin but please don't turn up without an appointment and in fact as far as I can tell they don't even bother to have a website. We will be shown around with great pride by a younger member of the family, Pierre Boillot, a very knowledgeable wine maker who knows intimately the parcels of land in the villages providing the grapes for his high quality wine. Villages whose names are a famous roll call of French wine such as Volnay, Pommard, Fixin, Nuits Saint Georges, Beaune and of course Gevrey Chambertin. These are all names famous around the world and all on the easy to follow Route des Vins that takes you around these gentle slopes. The wines for tasting here are chiefly reds, much deeper, fruitier, more complex and richer than the reds of Northern Burgundy. We have a generous and fascinating tasting, encountering wines that are at the high end of the possibilities of production from these famous lands. They taste expensive, they are not wines that will be offered on some '25% mix six bottles' reduction back in a supermarket in England; these stand on their own and are sought after by connoisseurs around the world and they hold a high price. Pierre is a generous man and he makes his wine affordable to our party although the downside of that is in having to purchase younger wines that will need to be kept for some time before drinking to allow them to taste close to the very fine samples provided by Pierre in this ancient cellar deep in the village of Gevrey. I still have a bottle of his Pommard 1$^{st}$ Cru Les Fremiers (1999) and probably by now I should have drunk it. Not only is it a reminder of a wonderful visit but I just don't know if it is at perfection, there is a danger it is past peak perfection but I must open it soon.

Pommard is one of the best known appellations in Burgundy and you find the vineyards themselves just south of Beaune going on to Autun. The tiny village of Pommard is a place you will drive through in the blink of an eye. This is a pleasant spot with vineyards either side of the road, lovely stone walls of the region surrounding the fields. There are some character properties to view and also the large Château de Pommard, a magnificent domaine dating from 1726. Wine tasting and other experiences are available here but it is not a degustation establishment for a simple call in when you are passing.

We bid a reluctant farewell to Pierre, another step in our wine education is complete and we are learning fast. I for one have learnt that you must never go into a wine shop in Beaune unaccompanied, try and keep an expert close by you in this region.

Our second visit of the day would lead us nicely into our evening meal also. The domaine we were visiting is in the village of Santenay, south west of Beaune. The journey takes you through the Montrachet villages of Puligny and Chassagne, beautiful gently unspoilt landscape and architecture. Here we stopped at - Domaine Prieur Brunet, Ch. Perruchot rue de Narosse, 21590 Santenay. It is worth pointing out that if you are following some of the addresses in the book that Prieur Brunet has recently been acquired by the négociant Louis Jadot and tastings and purchase at this domaine may no longer be possible. On this day the tasting was generous and long with a tour of the vineyard itself as part of the treats on offer. At the side of the domaine property there is a huge mural on the gable end of a building showing the extent of the domaine and a view into the cellar where a tasting is being enjoyed. We too would now enjoy such a tasting in a characterful exposed stone walled room with old wooden barrels providing a backdrop. We are seated at a long oak table and provided with information about the domaine and the wines on offer but it is the tasting we are interested in and it soon gets underway. The Santaney reds are a little lighter than the Gevrey Chambertin examples of the morning and it is here that we first get a real sense of what the whites of Burgundy have to offer and their chardonnay white Burgundy is honey rich and mellow. The presentation of the tasting is a little technical in structure, there is a desire to help you to appreciate how the wine is produced, an explanation of the inevitable *terroir* and certainly a sense once more of the family tradition. We are learning a lot and the confidence this type of visit will give us holds us in good stead in the years to come.

It was here that Bob made his first serious attempt to interrogate the owners with some searching questions that obviously were not coming from any casual drinker of Burgundy. He got a reluctant answer to a couple of them but they got increasingly technical and the owner became protective and defensive and the subject was changed to something a little more simple like the bouquet of the wine. Bob was not to be discouraged and headed off into the fields to make a study of the vines and the soil. He is a very enthusiastic wine producer and eager to keep learning and I am sure he took a lot away from his visit to Burgundy and his wines now stand shoulder to shoulder with excellent wines from France.

We have not yet finished with Prieur Brunet

as tonight we are to dine at their restaurant in Santaney - Restaurant Le Terroir en Côte d'Or, 19, Place du Jet d'eau 21590 Santenay. The restaurant today perhaps has no actual connection with the domaine especially after the Jadot takeover but on our visit the food was a showcase for the wines of Prieur Brunet and would be long remembered although for Niamh it was an evening of discovery she would rather forget.

The restaurant is housed in a fine old stone building in the village and very attractive it is, immaculately furnished inside with crisp white tablecloths and shining cutlery and glasses. Outside there is a tempting terrace that looks out onto the village square with a large fountain dominating the space. You can look through the spray of water to the vineyards gently sloping on the hillside beyond. As Jane Austen would say: 'It is happily situated'. I can be quite specific about our menu tonight as it was so enjoyable I have kept a record of it:

Salade de saumon cru marine a l'huile    d'olive
Filet de loup de mer son lit de fin legumes, sauce chardonnay (Prieur Brunet)
Assiette de fromage: delice de Bourgogne,

epoisse, citeaux

Parfait glace au marc de Bourgogne

The Prieur Brunet wines complemented the meal superbly and it was a lovely relaxed evening in a setting that enhanced the whole occasion, a real taste of Burgundian hospitality.

Sadly Niamh found out that she had an allergy to samphire and spent an uncomfortable night with a stomach cramp reaction starting immediately she ate the samphire as an accompaniment to the fish and these symptoms got progressively worse until morning. It was nothing too serious but a lesson learnt to avoid this particular vegetable in the future. She was up and ready for more wine tasting in the morning however.

Our last morning in Beaune was a real treat and a privileged visit to one of Beaune's well known wine houses located in an atmospheric side street just by the ancient town walls – Maison Champy, 5 Rue du Grenier À Sel, 21200 Beaune. Champy have a boutique in the centre of Beaune close by the L'Hôtel Dieu but we were able to go to their site in town where they have cellars under the ancient streets. Maison Champy have been wine producers in the region since 1720 and the cellars as we will see certainly reflect that history and tradition in the old town. Champy have access to some of the finest sites in the Cote d'Or and Cote d'Nuits. The list of named wines available from their cellar are from the top quality villages in the region. We were in expert hands here and this morning would really add to our knowledge and understanding of this most complex of wine regions. The tasting room is dominated by a very large old wooden barrel stood on its end and into which two copper bowls for spitting the wine are secured – I have to say our party does not waste the wine and these are never used.

Our host for the tasting was an immaculately dressed young lady who knew her subject down to the finest detail. The French take their wine and the presentation of it very seriously in these grand old wine houses. By contrast in the countryside you may get the vigneron himself breaking away from his work in the fields, dusting himself down and grabbing a few bottles to happily give you a degustation. Here in Beaune at these important maisons of wine everything is gleaming and crisp and our young host presents herself as befitting the status of the wines she will show us. Hanging on her every word our party enjoy a superb tasting and it does seem that the soft and delicate tones of her French accent actually elevate the wine in your mouth to another level – maybe I am being a bit romantic about that but the wines are extremely fine, at the top of the range in quality. The prices as expected reflect that but there is no way that people are not going to leave without a bottle or two. I feel sorry for our American friends who cannot take very much back with them but they purchase a fine bottle to pack into their suitcase for home. We content ourselves with two wines – a 2001 Chablis Premier cru Cote de Lechet and expensively a treat for our friends around the dining table is a 2001 Corton Grand Cru. The reds of course are relying on the pinot noir grape and back in the UK we tend to associate that with some fairly unremarkable and relatively cheap imports from around the world. The level of quality that the French in Burgundy elevate it to is a totally different wine and these wines available in Maison Champy are never going to be a cheap import. The tradition and *terroir* are there for all to appreciate and once again it is a chance to see the difference between villages that are producing the same grapes and even the difference between parcels of land in the same village. It is also an opportunity to really grasp how age affects a wine and the effect of weather conditions in any particular year – we are learning a lot and it is all very interesting and I want to learn more and so we will.

Our visit here is not restricted to a tasting and we are handed over by the young lady to a man who is dressed a little less beautifully – we are off to the cellars deep below the cobbled streets and this is a rare privilege and one of the benefits of being on a guided tour in this more inaccessible region. The cellars here at Champy are truly astonishing and steeped in the long history of this wine house. It seems that nothing has ever changed down here, the wooden storage racks that appear to have fossilized to stone are from the 18$^{th}$ century. The walls are musty and full of spreading wine mould. There are cases of wine all along the passageways and hidden in dark alcoves beneath the low ceilings. The really astonishing part is looking at the loose bottles down here in the cellars. Some of these are very old vintages and it is not surprising to see many bottles still available from between the wars. Actually when you start to explore farther down the passages these bottles are in fact relatively young.

We come across an 1898 Volnay, 1875 Pommard and oldest of all a Chambertin from 1858 – this is a real treat to see and we are all in awe at what is down here. There are old 20th century vintages set in antique wooden racks. These bottles are completely encased in dust and mould and would require much attention and relabelling to get ready for sales to someone who would have to be a very serious collector with bottomless pockets. As we emerge back above into the light we all feel a long way removed from being home and selecting a bottle in the supermarket or wine store. We have seen a totally different side to wine and its production and indeed what can be done with the noble grape. Life will never be the same again but I will continue to refuse to become a wine snob which you could so easily do.

It is time to leave Beaune and move on to Beaujolais where we will stay in the village of Villié-Morgon and the Hotel Villon, finding more new gems in an area that is relatively underrepresented in the UK other than the Beaujolais Nouveau that of course everyone knows.

# BEAUJOLAIS

Beaujolais is a beautiful region of rolling hills, some quite small, almost mounds really with vineyards on the slopes. The land is formed with a base of granite and limestone and as you would expect the *'terroir'* is distinctive. Beaujolais is an easily recognisable wine with a character much different from its near neighbour Burgundy, again showing how interesting it is to travel and taste your way through so many contrasting regions of France. The wines here in Beaujolais flow down to Lyon in the same way as the rivers that pass through that dramatic city and are part of the gastronomic culture that makes the city a French capital of food. We gain a very clear idea of what we will see in this area just from our hotel room window looking out over these gentle hills and vineyards It is a view that is worth every penny of the cost of a stay here – peaceful and bucolic. Villié-Morgon is an ideal location to base our stay and we will sleep soundly and eat well in this charming location.

Our first visit is to the Geoffray family of Château Thivin, 630 route du Mont Brouilly, 69460 ODENAS. This domaine is chiefly known for the Côte de Brouilly and Brouilly crus, an appellation that this house was instrumental in creating.

They make a claim to have the most magnificent vineyards in Beaujolais and who am I to argue as we look around the panorama from this stunning location stretched out in front of the ancient château. It is a grand old building steeped in history and one that changed hands after the French Revolution and moving into the ownership of the Geoffray family in 1877. It is one of their young descendants Claude Edouard Geoffray who will show us around the family property.

The fascinating tasting room has its own St Vincent statue standing in an old stone alcove set into the deep walls. It is an altar to the patron saint of wine and I imagine a few prayers have been said in front of this image to encourage favourable weather conditions. Once again here at Château Thivin the cellars are ancient and extensive, the walls thick with moulded age. They are fascinating and the history is thoroughly explained to us as like all growers in this region they are immensely proud of their heritage. The caves go on and on with a network of pipes and pre-war electrics lining the walls. It takes a small step of imagination to sense that much would have been hidden in these cellars in the time of Vichy France and the occupation. No doubt some people also hid away deep below ground.

There is plenty of testimony to the modernisation of the château operation but they have not thrown away the past. On display is a wonderful old wooden wine press with a heavy iron corkscrew. Alongside it and still in use is a marvellous Heath Robinson piece of 1930's engineering that is still used to filter the wine. Claude Edouard has studied wine production extensively and observed methods around the world as far away as New Zealand. He will go on to take the domaine farther in partnership with his parents and future wife ensuring that the domaine remains in very safe hands.

The tasting is in two parts, a simple one in the cellar area to complement our tour below ground and a more instructive one by Claude Edouard in the tasting room where we are comfortably sat at a long table set out with white tablecloths, gleaming domaine glasses and freshly baked bread that will absorb the wine. The room contains a large variety of old objects that have been used over the years on the domaine. There are wooden plaques stamped with past vintages adorning the antique wooden beams that hold up the timbered roof. The more you look round the domaine the more Saint Vincent's you see – Château Thivin takes no chances.

The wine we select for home is Cuvée Zaccharie, Côte-De-Brouilly red, named after an ancestor in the family of course. This fine wine is produced from gamay noir vines that are around 50 years old and grown on the slopes of Colline de Brouilly, a stony clay based well drained slope that ultimately produces this beautiful wine. The wine is deep and fruity, with an aroma of very ripe blackberries and has been aged for nine months in oak barrels. I imagine this being opened back home in winter with an accompanying cheese board. I am sure that Lancashire cheese would be a perfect compliment.

Despite these wines being deep and full bodied they are much lighter than most Burgundy wines. It is amazing just how different the regions are despite being near neighbours. Often the wines here in Beaujolais are drunk just slightly chilled and in cafés and restaurants your carafe will be presented to the table at less than room temperature.

One thing that all are unspokenly agreed on is that this location of Château Thivin is glorious. All the party are silently standing around and taking in the panorama spread out before us. The vineyards stretching out beyond us are a rich deep green now and an old tractor and trailer is being slowly manoeuvred through the vines as the workers check the growth. The view is unspoilt. You can take yourself back in time and Château Thivin is the perfect example of a place at one with its *terroir*, a marriage of new production ideas blended with rich tradition. It is a visit that will live long in the memory as my writing about it today testifies.

For a change the afternoon is spent mainly in sightseeing and we are able to take lunch at our leisure in Macon and admire the Saône river that passes through the city. My only previous encounter with Macon was stopping at the autoroute services in the middle of the night on a coach journey to the south. It is a far more pleasant experience to wander through the ancient streets and find a delightful restaurant with a small outside terrace. A lovely spot for our lunch. The food here is locally produced with freshwater fish from the rivers, snails from the vineyards and the main event from this region – the aristocratic chickens from nearby Bresse. There is plenty to see in Macon and it is especially pleasing to any lover of architecture with an abundance of old churches and municipal buildings. The bridge over the Saône is quite a sight. If you have the time then the view back to the city from the opposite bank is well worth the effort. After leaving the restaurant and heading down the hill back to the quayside I suddenly realised why the lady looked bemused and amused as I left her. I had mixed up a few words of French and ascribed a totally different meaning to my attempt at conversation. I was too embarrassed to go back and explain but perhaps if I leave it long enough she will not remember me.

We move on to the town of Cluny, a place that is famous for a $10^{th}$ century abbey that despite its woes following the French Revolution still dominates the landscape and is the reason for most people's visit to the town. The parts of the abbey we see today date from the 1100's and the fine cloister is from around 1760. The parts that remain include the towers and from these a majestic view of Cluny and the surrounding countryside can be enjoyed. Because of the claimed presence of the relics of Saint Peter and Saint Paul it enabled Cluny to be for two centuries from 910 when the monastery was founded to be second only to Rome in religious power and influence in Europe during that time. The abbots from Cluny used that status effectively and were important players on the international political scene. That influence waned and after the Revolution the Abbey was sold and much of it including the Romanesque church was demolished. It remains a very atmospheric place however and enough building remains to give a sense of the importance of this sacred site.

The streets around the abbey that make up this village are very pretty and attractive, ancient side streets, some with steps leading up to the higher parts of the village that are enticing and great photo opportunities.

Cluny has another claim to fame and it is an unexpected one. If you have any interest in equine matters then the French National horse breeding centre is located here - the 'Haras National'. Here they breed and train pure bred stock and these buildings can be visited. Even if you do not go inside you will see plenty of examples of these magnificent equine specimens being exercised and ridden around the streets of Cluny. It adds a quite surreal air to the village, a genuine step back in time and it is all very elegant and precise. The buildings of the Haras National are extensive and recall the time of Napoleon and French military history when the horse was king and battles were won and lost on the quality of the horse and the skill of its rider. We will return to Cluny a few years later and enjoy a visit that coincided with a horse show in the grounds and that was most impressive. To just come to an area and only partake of the wine is not telling the entire story and by taking in the towns and villages and their history it helps towards understanding that illusive '*terroir*'.

Before we move on with the wine tour let us have a brief interlude from earlier in the tour.

# MAXIMES

I didn't tell you earlier about our real stars of the wine tour, our couple Emma and Richard who have the world revolving around them. So much so that they nearly caused an international incident on our evening meal taken as a group in Auxerre. Le Maxime is a lovely, old established hotel restaurant on the banks of the Yonne, set below the town, overlooked by the ancient cathedral and abbey. The walk down from our hotel is an exploratory interesting wind down through the medieval streets and architecture. This early evening walk is very pleasing and appealing as you meander down the attractive cobbled streets towards the river, going past many fine ancient timbered houses. You cannot miss the beautiful churches. Cathédrale Saint-Étienne is the most striking of these with its worryingly damaged façade, although it will have substantial renovation devoted to it in the intervening years. I digress, but Auxerre is well worth a few days of your time especially with good company, although assuredly tonight that good standard will be sorely tested. Joan of Arc visited the town on two occasions and tonight I really wished she had still been around, we needed her help.

Emma and Richard had stood aloof from the rest of the party during the vineyard visits with just one or two of us making occasional forays into their space to basically see what they are about and try to engage with them. It appears that they are indeed a couple, of sorts. She has a home in the Ribble Valley in Lancashire quite near to where we live and is a professional person but we will never know exactly the field in which she practices. He is from and lives in Surrey, again even more of a professional. We would soon find out he certainly was a 'professional'. He is clearly from his own considered opinion very important to the ongoing best workings of the human race and she concurs. They teasingly endeavour to give off an air of mystery about their exact relationship and delight in trying to tantalise the company about it.

Truth is we couldn't care less.

Once in their space we give our poor excuse for intelligent conversation, always difficult when the other party know everything and can also speak properly, not like Lancashire folk. To be fair they initially in a conversation are quite affable and seem likely to be good company but the problem arises when you express an opinion however small and on however inconsequential a subject. It is then that you are immediately made to feel a very small, ignorant, stupid person and it is made clear you have offended them deeply. Their arrogance and lack of regard for anyone's feelings is breath-taking. You are forced to slink away mortally wounded in spirit and pity the next person that tries to engage with them. I know it is said Yorkshiremen 'call a spade a spade' but this response is hitting you over the head with the spade as well.

Tonight we are late, our afternoon wine tour overran as is to be expected when you taste at least eight wines in enthusiastic company and the winemaker is so taken by our increasing expressions of joy at each new wine that he continues by bringing out the wines reserved for family and special friends. After such a copious tasting you really are special friends or so the wine is telling you.

We arrive at Maximes getting on for an hour late and understandably the a la carte option for such a large group is no longer available. The host kindly explains that the chef will have to offer a fixed menu now for a group of twenty five as he cannot prepare so many courses with choice in the time available. We all understand and even though just as in the Fawlty Towers sketch it seems to be a bit like duck in three superbly different ways we all hungrily accept. Except for two.

Oh no, they have rights, they have paid for this, they are going to have exactly what they expected.

Oh and by the way this is exactly what you would expect of the French.

They were happy to accept plenty of wine and hospitality this afternoon however. The pomposity of it all is beginning to reverberate right back to the British shores and the embarrassment amongst our party is palpable. No one knows where to look but these two are only just warming up. The fat lady is not even clearing her throat.

Finally they accept with very little good grace that it has to be this way, short of them going out on their own and finding another restaurant but even they can appreciate it is getting late. So duck all round for our merry band. Unfortunately Niamh and I along with another couple of weary travellers are on the deadly duos table and tonight is going to be some experience and certainly not in a good way.

Memorable it will be.

When the first course comes it is duck as expected but marinated and cured in a salad, quite raw to an English palate. This does not go down well and the grumpy factor level is rising. The dish is in fact delicious and there can be no complaints.

Obviously with our two there are. There is a water problem, yes a water problem. That essentially tasteless substance we know and love. Tonight we have a connoisseur of H2o. She wanted Badoit sparking water and guess what, they only have Evian. To me water is not an area that is worth being a connoisseur in but she goes absolutely ballistic on the subject of this pathetic excuse for a restaurant as she sees it. On and on she rants at the poor waitress and then to the owner about how ridiculous it is that they don't offer Badoit. How can they possibly claim to be a serious restaurant. Badoit is THE mineral water and nothing else should be offered by a proper self-respecting restaurant. On and on she rants, standing toe to toe with the owner and the bemused waitress. Sadly for her she eventually has to accept that there is no Badoit and never will be, certainly not tonight, although I have a feeling the owner might start stocking a bottle or two.

From this moment on whenever we are eating in France and especially with friends this has become a standing joke every time we order water. Once in a Paris restaurant a friend ordered Badoit and I laughed and said 'you will be lucky'. It did seem that it would never be served and we were laughing so hard when it eventually arrived at the table that the waiter must have thought we were crazy English people. I have a picture of my friend with his hard earned bottle. Some people just have to have their Badoit.

Everyone in the Auxerre restaurant is now is so very uneasy and the atmosphere in the room, the lovely friendly Maximes, is toxic. Still be assured the fat lady is still silent, we ain't seen nothing yet.

Anyway, we had misheard about it being duck all the way as it turns out to be steak as a main course. This cheers everyone up except the vegetarians but what is this we hear stirring with our beautiful couple of diplomats once again.

Part of the meal deal was a reasonable quantity of wine on the house i.e. a bottle between two and any more wine needed to be ordered and paid for. This arrangement seemed fair enough to 95% of us. This is not the case with our friends on the table. No, they felt that a fair quantity really equated to exactly how much they were able to drink in a session. Having previously quaffed eight glasses of wine in the afternoon half a bottle seemed to me not just sufficient but sensible for our long term health.

Whatever had gone before was a real minor breath of wind compared to the tornado of abuse Richard was about to unleash. The tour guide got the initial volley but then the owner came over with the sommelier and that is when he really got into his stride. Fortunately, or should I say unfortunately, I knew enough French to understand that what he was spewing out in his perfect public school French was the foulest abuse imaginable. Proper 18 (R) certificate stuff. In fact I doubt it would have got past any censor. The room otherwise was silent with the rest of the party wishing the ground would open up. To their credit the French did not retaliate but they should probably have ordered them out. There now was played out in the restaurant the most bizarre and totally unexpected scene, a real French farce.

As far as we knew our wine tour was the only one taking place in the region at that time.

Then, suddenly and dramatically, the tour guide burst through the scene and ran into the adjoining room which was hidden behind closed doors. She emerged seconds later with a man whom we recognized as the owner of the wine tour company. He had in fact been running a second wine tour alongside ours. We had this bizarre spectacle of a middle aged, thoroughly well lubricated man, his wine stained white shirt hanging outside his trousers, wine themed tie still loosely clinging to his neck, wading unsteadily into battle. He had clearly enjoyed a very, very good day. Speaking with his well-bred posh English accent, an accent somewhat slurred to a degree, he cut a very weird figure indeed. He staggered into the group, dislodging a couple of bar stools on the way, trying to spread bonhomie to the embattled host. He was all the while trying not to hit them with the almost empty bottle of red Cotes de Beaune held in his left hand whilst brushing back his unruly Boris Johnson style hair. Even our indignant self-righteous couple realised that the argument could not go on with him in this condition as he would never comprehend it anyway. His only thought was to spread goodwill and get back to his party and uncork another bottle. Without any further ado he prized the wallet from his pocket and waved a large quantity of French francs at the poor abused owner and ordered a vat of wine for everyone.

So the French and English averted war on this occasion and somehow the non-duck dessert course passed off peacefully but I could not help feeling that the dessert served to Richard and Emma probably had one or two bonus ingredients in it. Thankfully they did not order coffee and left the restaurant together before anyone else. We all then had a wonderful twenty minutes without them to end a spectacularly awful evening but as I said before, it was memorable.

# POUILLY-FUISSÉ & THE EBULLIENT M.ROY

It is most difficult to pick out a highlight from this wine tour and our continuing education but today produced two absolute gems. They are domaines that we will return to on our own with our new found confidence and wine knowledge to taste and purchase when we tour the vineyards of France by car. Our first stop today is in the village of Montagny-le-Buxy - Château de la Saule, 71390 MONTAGNY-LES-BUXY. This is the family home of Alain Roy, a most extraordinary man whose passion for the wines of his vineyards and the area of his birth will leave you breathless and exhausted (in a good way). The château is a most attractive place, the elegant house built to a scale that feels homely and comfortable. The buildings are surrounded by beautifully tended grounds and of course vineyards – it is a romantic place. Over many generations the domaine has traditionally grown chardonnay grapes to produce the Montagny AOC but M.Roy also now has a patch of land that produces pinot noir and this red would be one of our purchases on this visit.

Alain Roy, a man in his late fifties on this visit, is a livewire of a man, a veritable Duracell bunny if you are familiar with the English long life battery advert. His enthusiasm is unquenchable and he is constantly on the move during his extravagant presentation to us, thinking ahead to the next topic and the next bottle, his beaming face projecting the most affable of men. Alongside him he has a extremely attractive assistant with whom he appears to engage in a flirtatious double act that she is finding difficult to keep up with and she at times is convulsed in laughter. Never have I tasted wine in such a setting and M.Roy has the confidence and delivery of a showman and he knows that this is one production we will never forget.

The vast quantities of as yet unfilled glasses set out on a long table by his young lady testify that this is going to be a generous tasting and so it proves to be.

There are three wines that M.Roy wishes to display to us, ones that will show the beauty of a wine that is not often seen in the UK although these are available if you look hard enough and are well worth seeking out - Montagny 1er Cru Cuvée Classique, Montagny 1er Cru "Cuvée Fût and Montagny 1er Cru Les Burnins. However, in a way that is similar to my feelings about Sancerre, these are wines that are at their best tasted in the region and climate of production. The best of the wines are surely, as is the case with Sancerre, held in reserve here in France. The production is quite limited in any case so there are not vast quantities available for export. It is I assure you a very fine wine and Alain Roy is a genius in producing such a gorgeous chardonnay. The land is clay and mineral and that comes through in the bouquet and taste of these white wines along with flowery and fruity notes. The taste is somewhat reminiscent of the wines of Pouilly-Fuissé. They are a little gold in colour with a greenish tinge but turn lighter with ageing and they can be kept for a few years. These wines are superb, they just have to be as no one can be this enthusiastic about a product that is not exceptional. M.Roy is very enthusiastic, probably feeling that there are absolutely no finer white wines in all of France and who am I to argue. He has the audience here in his wonderful stone cellar in the palm of his hand and even if we do not understand all that he is saying during his repartee with his glamourous assistant we are spellbound with his performance and the undoubted quality of his wine. Another excellent purchase for home and the English winter and I am so looking forward to serving these with some fresh fish or just as an aperitif. M.Roy is not finished with us yet. We will be entertained further by him as he has provided the most excellent buffet lunch under the shade of the trees around his courtyard.

No better setting could there be – all is very well with the world today. I have a feeling that we will all need a siesta following the tasting and partaking of this most generous supply of local produce set out before us.

The tables are arranged under the shade of a row

of old walnut trees and the buffet table set farther back to give maximum shade and a little coolness in the heat of the day. Jack and Hilary, our new found American friends come to sit with us and of course my faithful companion Henry is by my side. The party is a very eclectic mix of people but an interesting one and each one of us in their own way seems to find common ground – there are of course one or two exceptions but there is always a spare table for them. Henry is one of those very gentle people who are interesting when they can express themselves but find social interaction for the most part a difficult and painful experience. He is enjoying the trip and I am happy to be his 'comfort blanket' as it were but I do feel sad for him that he is fighting his demons constantly. Jack and Hilary by contrast are never short of conversation and this trip you sense is like a dream come true for them. They have travelled father than anyone and are completely entranced by what they have found here in Burgundy.

The buffet spread is superb and the whole outdoor picnic reminds me of the times of the Impressionists who would no doubt have gathered under the shade of a tree in Monet's garden and had a long lingering lunch accompanied by plenty of wine before settling for an afternoon siesta. Painting a canvas or two in the gentle late afternoon light would follow as another carafe of chilled white eased them into the evening.

We are in an idyllic spot and M.Roy works all the tables with wine bottle in hand, no one will go home hungry or thirsty today and we will always remember this remarkable man. His wines are at their finest in the warmth of the shade of the trees with such fine local produce to accompany and compliment them.

The day for Jack and Hilary is already memorable but for Hilary is will shortly become unforgettable and not in a way she was expecting. M.Roy and his lovely assistant have set out on a table beside us a range of fruits including some succulent local strawberries and these have attracted the local population of bees and wasps. They are not bothering us unduly as they seem happy with the occasional nibble at the fruit. They seem unconcerned with our lunch plates but then one of the wasps breaks off from the feast and flies straight onto Hilary's loaded fork. She initially is unaware of it and takes this mouthful into her mouth but the cornered wasp reacts and bites her on the tongue. She is in agony and shock and the concern is that it will bite her throat and cause breathing problems. She seems to be struggling to get her breath. Fortunately we do have a couple in the party who are qualified to handle the situation and they manage to calm Hilary down and affect a remedy with the help of M.Roy. Hilary is in discomfort for the rest of the day and it will spoil her enjoyment of the rest of the visit and the evening meal but it could have been worse. I learnt a non-wine related lesson here and will always from now on when talking still keep my eyes peeled for any flying creature coming near my food.

This has been a fabulous visit with such splendid and generous hospitality and we will never forget it. The Montagny wines were a revelation. We would enjoy them back home. As we all gathered up our cases of wine the large boot of the coach became ever more chock-full. I purchased two wines that particularly impressed: Montagny 1st Cru White and Montagny Ist Cru White Fut de Chene. I also took home a case of M.Roy's new venture with red wines from a parcel of land that comes under the Givry appellation, a 2002 vintage. Givry is a relatively light, fresh red wine and is drunk young rather than being left to age in the cellar. The Givry is a lovely wine to drink on its own on a warm summer's day in the garden. The village of Givry is ancient and the production of wine here dates back to the Middle Ages when it was a very important supplier to the connoisseurs of Paris. Château Saule Roy I wholeheartedly commend to you and if you are ever in this lovely, gentle area then do pay M.Roy a visit. I know you will be warmly welcomed.

We say our reluctant goodbyes but we do need to move on as we have another highlight of our trip to experience and it is one we have all been eagerly looking forward to – Château Fuissé in the village of that name who produce the famous wines designated Pouilly-Fuissé. The wines here are personally ones that I feel are the finest in the region and if you are a lover of white wine then this part of France is arguably as good as it gets. We will return here on our own in years to come and it is without question my favourite wine although Sancerre will probably still carry the day for Niamh.

The villages are to the west of the Autoroute and the E62 converges with three or four other roads and the TGV railway. This convergence is called Pattie D'Oie or goosefoot and there is a restaurant of that name at this location. The scenery here is gentle and you do feel that the local residents most certainly have their paradise with the hills gently sloping around the scene of the five communes that are able to call their wines Pouilly-Fuissé. It is as fine a view as you will find in all of France with the soft, ancient limestone walls bearing testament to the type of *terroir* in the region. The soft slopes contain the chardonnay vineyards and these are harvested later than most in the Burgundy region, giving the resulting grapes more sugar content. We will find that the village of Loché also gives a beautiful wine called Pouilly-Loché. Throughout this region the parcels of land are quite small and distinctive. It is a blessed land and the produce from it is to be treasured and savoured. We are anticipating this visit expectantly.

The visit on this occasion to the captivating Château Fuissé will be a genuine highlight of the trip and we are overwhelmed by the warm welcome and the beauty of this location. The château and domaine are owned by the Vincent family.

Their involvement in wine production and in fact in gaining the appellation of Pouilly-Fuissé for the region back in the 1920's placed them at the forefront of makers. The château itself has a homely feel to it, not being too large and impersonal but it is still extremely impressive. The gentle gradients of the vineyards surrounding the château all seem to lead to the house itself as if the wine would just pour into the courtyard and into the barrels. It is a place that is totally at one with its surroundings and could only be destined to be used for one purpose – wine. The room generally used for tasting is in the courtyard and quite atmospheric but today we are privileged to be taken into the château itself to a grand room that rolls back the years of history. For a moment or two our eyes are all drawn to the room itself with its glorious ceiling and grand fireplace. Just briefly our gaze is diverted to the array of glasses and wine bottles set out on the large oak table. You feel quite special to have been allowed into this glorious space and you cannot help but feel that the wine is going to taste that much better in the historical context of the château. I am not wrong on that score. The château of course is famous for the Pouilly-Fuissé production but the Vincent family have much more to offer from parcels of land that give fine examples of Saint-Véran, Mâcon-Villages, Mâcon-Fuissé, Bourgogne-Blanc, and even some Juliénas. In total they have access to more than one hundred parcels of land in the region, all producing high quality wines including a range bottled under the Vincent name. They know the parcels of vineyards intimately and their sense of *terroir* extends to adapting the vinification to suit the respective personalities of each area. When you stand in the courtyard you get a sense of the quality and tradition of the land as you see that the vineyards come right up to the château enabling you to examine the luscious grapes at close quarters. Before we are taken to see the *'terroir'* itself we must have a tasting and this is given by the charming wife of the current family manager of the Domaine. She is so generous with her offering of wines to us and in sharing her love of the Domaine itself.

The tasting takes place under the watchful eyes of the medieval characters on a beautiful tapestry hanging behind the table on the exposed stone wall of the room. To one side there is a full size suit of armour and some ancient tools of the wine maker's trade adorn the walls behind. It is difficult to concentrate on the wine due to the interesting and beautiful setting but our host encourages us to approach the table and indulge in the real reason for our visit. Some of our party are taking advantage of the sumptuous chairs in the room, particular either side of the imposing fireplace, to sit and have a moment of contemplation but even they eventually move over to the long oak table. We are taken mainly through the Pouilly-Fuissé wines and also the Saint-Véran and it is enlightening once again to be able to taste and smell the differences between the parcels of land, how the *terroir* and production methods change the complexity of the finished product.

Choosing wines to take home is going to be difficult, the château wines are quite expensive but offered at prices that bear no relation to what we would pay back home. There are clear favourites. The stand out wine for me is the one that sees its vines almost creeping into the château itself – Le Clos. The stone walls of Le Clos surround the Château de Fuissé and inside the ancient walls are growing vieilles vignes or old vines which are all over fifty years old. They produce an extraordinary wine that is pale and golden although with a hint of green. It is a wine that when chilled you can just imagine the pleasure of drinking with seafood or a firm piece of grilled Cornish turbot. The French would also feel that this is perfect for accompanying charcuterie, such as a sausage made from the rest of the wild boar whose mounted head resides over the fireplace. However, I will enjoy this wine simply with fish back home. We also buy a basic Pouilly-Fuissé and two other very fine examples: Pouilly-Fuissé Les Brules, a mineral rich wine and Pouilly-Fuissé Les Combettes, another example of the effect of the limestone soil.

Reluctantly we have to make our way out of this beguiling room as our host leads us back to the courtyard and she kindly allows us to go into the vineyard of Le Clos and absorb the attractive scene of the vines extending in perfectly tended neat rows up the dry, stony slopes. It is a truly magical place and you do have the feeling that with such perfect produce right on your doorstep that you cannot fail but create great wines. It is of course not that simple and the Vincent family can only do this by respecting the traditions and skills of all the generations that have gone before them and throughout this region you cannot escape the importance of heritage and the knowledge that has been handed down.

This is a region that we returned to often in the coming years and perhaps I can divert you from wine and share with you just one of those visits that can give you a flavour of what you can find in this quiet, unspoilt area. I will include some wine visits of course but also a little more of the delights you will find in touring gently around the countryside and villages. I will keep this recollection in more of a blog style of writing which I hope you will enjoy.

# RURAL BURGUNDY & BEAUJOLAIS

We had made the journey from Provence to Azé in Burgundy. What a contrast this is to the area around Nice on the Cotes D'Azur as the only sound appears to be cows in the fields gently munching on the lush green grass.

We have a super room here at La Portail Bleus, 10 rue de Montchanin, 71260 Azé and had a lovely welcome from Steve and Linda (now run by a young Dutch couple who still get great reviews) with a welcoming pot of tea. This is going to be a contrast of B & B's with this one seeming very homely in the sense that you feel you are staying right in someone's home. We had arrived from La Surprise in Provence, a place that gave you more of an independent space but here in Burgundy the sociable Steve and Linda clearly revel in having guests around them. I hope we can stay awake properly for them tonight at the dinner table after our long day of travelling.

Dinner is a really well cooked affair and most enjoyable, chicken sautéed in a garlic and wine sauce and the best bit of all a really superb homemade tarte au citron. Linda is a fine cook. Steve was very generous with the local wines which we were more than happy to discover. Azé appends its name to a lovely white Burgundy from a small appellation.

The other guests amazingly are from near to where we live in Lancashire and Mike actually works for the council in the same town I work in. We mutually know many people in the council but I will not hold that against him. I came here to forget some ongoing business battles back home with the powers that be. It is a very small world.

Linda regaled us with this story about an armed robbery in the village at the local épicerie that occurred only last week. This seemed about as likely as saying the locals were going to work through their lunch tomorrow. However the next day the papers told of the capture of the gang in Macon, apparently a group of Moroccan immigrants. We have certainly been aware on this trip that the French are chafing at this perceived change in the makeup of the population and clearly believe that it contributes to a new type of, and increase, in crime. A few tensions are in the air without a doubt.

We slept incredibly well before being awoken around 5.30 by tremendous noise in the street outside. There is a very large food and artisan fair here this weekend and workers had arrived to block the road and start work on the stands. Apart from the noise, they caused mayhem as the French obviously don't believe 'route barree' means what is says and large lorries ended up being turned back and having to reverse in the narrow road.

Again, only in France.

Wednesday 27th July

After breakfast we headed to Pont de Vaux where Linda said there was an excellent market. It certainly was a real French market that was in no way geared to the tourist, in sharp contrast to some popular markets in Provence. It was really enjoyable to stroll around the market but sadly though we were not in a position to buy any produce as we have no cooking facilities here. There are lots of chicken rotisserie stalls and they offered a superb aroma, the local chicken of course being the best in France - Bresse, with its own appellation just like the wine. The fresh chickens had their tell-tale metal tag on the leg and they were wrapped and labelled with a lot of pride and care.

The town has a marina on the canal that runs through the town and this made for a pleasant stroll. You can hire boats here and also take a guided trip on the canal.

We were having a problem with our car and this turned out to be the sump cover having come loose and consequently dragging on the floor. The mechanic at the first garage I found did not speak any English and I am not really sure that he spoke French either. It turned out they were just an auto electrical garage. The next one was a Peugeot garage and the guy said he could look at it if I would wait for him to deal with a couple of customers.

He soon had my vehicle on the ramp and sorted the problem, brought it down and drove it back out to us and then amazingly refused any payment. This was very kind of him and certainly not the service I am used to at garages in England. I gave him a bottle of wine for his trouble (I always have some lying around) and we thanked him very much for his helpfulness and generosity.

Off we then went to Cluny and headed for the centre square for a lunch stop. We decided on a brasserie, Café du Centre which provided excellent bistro cooking with extremely generous portions. Niamh had the plat du jour of lamb brochettes and I had a very large steak frites. With no room for desert we just had coffee and enjoyed the very Frenchness of such a place. Excellent.

Cluny is a very absorbing place to spend at least half a day. It had a few exhibitions taking place with pottery artisans and artists and of course you have the Abbey and many other buildings that are well worth a look. Today there was also a large equestrian event at the large showground in Cluny. We spent a couple of hours watching the events which were a French national horse championship. On show were some very fine horses, all handled with considerable skill. It made for a very pleasant afternoon.

There appeared to be a thunderstorm brewing from behind the arena and we decided to head back to the car and then to get a few provisions from the centre of Cluny to construct a snack in the evening.

The storm passed by and it turned into a very pleasant warm evening as we sat out with a bottle of the local white Macon-Perronne, not a wine we see in England.

We were joined later by Gavin and Vanessa who were South Africans staying here with their two children before heading south. Also staying was a sole traveller called Stacy from San Francisco. I felt it was very brave to do that and she had been away from home for a couple of weeks already. She also was heading east and south now to complete her journey.

Once again we slept soundly but knew we needed a quick shower in the morning as the French workmen were going to arrive early to dig up the road and mend a fast flowing leak. The water pressure is already low because of it and they will be turning it off completely. At least we did not have drills in the night.

## Thursday 29th July

Today is dull and the heavy skies look certain to provide rain. We head off to Beaujolais and first of all to Fuisse village to buy some Pouilly-Fuissé. We have bought from Château Fuisse before so decided on a change this time around. After a brief look around the village we settled on Domaine Roger Luquet, 101 Rue du Bourg, 71960 Fuissé. We were welcomed by a French speaking vigneron who began our tasting. He passed us over to a colleague who arrived into the room as she spoke some English. She guided us through a St Veran and some Pouilly-Fuissé. We bought the 2008 Pouilly-Fuissé and some St Veran, both excellent value compared to purchasing these back at home. She explained the 2009 tasted different to other years due to the weather conditions. This was in fact very different and virtually unrecognisable as Pouilly-Fuissé whereas the 2008 was very typical.

From there we headed around the villages, St Amour, Chenas, Julianas, Chitoubles, Fleurie and so on.

After a bit of a circuit we ended up back in Fleurie and went to the exceptional cave cooperative in the village. Inside were some local men who were not exactly dressed for the occasion but they looked like typical wine growers, men of the land. They appeared to be very settled and propping up the bar really rather than having an educational tasting. The lady welcomed us and after we had had a good look around the cellar we had an excellent tasting before buying a couple of different bottles, a fine Fleurie and a St Amour.

As we headed in search of lunch it clearly was going to start raining with a vengeance so we wisely went back towards Cluny. As we arrived it became torrential rain and people who had been eating 'en terrace' were scattering for cover with their sodden plates. The narrow streets were flowing like rivers as we parked up but we were trapped in the car for nearly half an hour before it was possible to get out and into the town. We dived into a local wine cave that we had seen the day before that served wine by the glass with a selection of tapas.

The only place available for us to sit was actually in the cave itself and we ate there at a high table surrounded by hundreds of bottles of expensive Burgundies. The light lunch was really excellent with rillettes, tapenade, choritzo, vegetables and jambon persillé washed down with Pouilly-Fuissé and a Morgan red. Followed by coffee this was just what was needed at a very reasonable price.

So after a stroll around Cluny we went back to the B & B to pack and to head out later for some dinner.

We had been recommended a local restaurant in the next village and as it was a Thursday we assumed it would not be busy. When we arrived we were early – it had a chalkboard sign saying open at 7.30. When it opened they said they were full – why put a sign up then! Frustrating!

We headed quickly over to Cluny but not much in the way of fine dining was open and the town was very quiet. There was nothing for it but to have a pizza – a good pizza – but still a pizza. Not the gourmet finish to our trip that we had hoped for – all dressed up with nowhere to go. It was a lesson learnt; if you really want to eat somewhere then always book.

Back at the B and B we joined the others and finished the communal wine before getting ready for the return trip.

Friday 29th July

We said our goodbyes after a really enjoyable stay here at La Portail Bleus. It felt like staying with friends and I would highly recommend it.

The journey home was amazing – we never encountered one hold up and arrived back in Lancashire at least two hours before expected. Another great trip successfully completed and we want to go back – now!

# COLLIOURE AND A CATALAN TREASURE

One of the great joys in travelling around France in search of excellent wine comes when you stumble across a small scale producer that would be unknown in the UK or your own country. It would be a producer that would be working in a way that was not high tech or promoted as a big business but using all the skill and knowledge of the land acquired over the decades or sometimes even centuries.

In a small wine shop located in a shady side

street just away from the harbour front in Collioure we had seen some bottles of local wine that had colourful artworks embellishing the labels. These were clearly not all appellation d'origine controlee production but wines produced in accord with the *terroir*, to the pleasing of the winemaker. They were distinctive and the colourful quirky labels screamed out the independent spirit of the maker. Although we could not try these wines in Collioure I managed to make out from the label the address of the domain and as it was more or less on our way back to our bed and breakfast stay we decided to pay them a call. As we journeyed away from our day by the Mediterranean coast at this stunningly beautiful town of Collioure we headed inland instead of driving through Perpignan, going across the A9 on the D612 to the small commune of Trouillas or Trullars if you wish to be popular with the Catalan locals. The area is very reminiscent of Northern Spain and particularly so with the landscape being dusty and parched from several weeks of hot sunny weather. The backdrop of the Pyrenees is spectacular and this mountain range dominates the plain that stretches along the coast to the Spanish border. This area has an historic claim to fame in that it was the scene of a famous battle in 1793 when the Spanish crossed the border for a skirmish at the Battle of Trouillas.

Located just outside the village we found the ancient mas - Chateau Mas Deu, a place that is so in tune with its setting. Driving up the dusty track we parked our car in the large open space in front of the mas. There are no frills here, no large glass fronted tasting room with expensive signage. This is authentic wine producing France, a place steeped in time and at one with its place in history. It is home to independent vignerons and proud of that fact. They have no pretentions to compete with the large scale producers of the region, many of them have sadly over the years given the area a poor reputation for quality. In writing up this recollection of a memorable visit I tried to find their website but it became apparent that they still do not have one. Life for them is not to be spent hovering over a keyboard and who can blame them.

It soon becomes clear why M.Claude Oliver does not have a website when you enter the cavernous tasting area and meet him. M.Oliver's passion is for wine and his beloved family that run the domain. It is also extremely obvious that perhaps rugby union is right at the top of his passions in life. Across the entire background of the cave are large flags of various rugby clubs and nations with pride of place going to the colours of his beloved Perpignan. Life for him is not to be lived in virtual reality but in the world of his vineyard, his family and most certainly the serious business of the rugby field. The area where you can have a degustation is the same area that houses all the vats and wooden casks containing the next vintage to be readied and bottled.

The welcome from M.Oliver is very warm and friendly, we feel like long lost friends as he guides us over to a table but not before he has noticed my interest in the rugby flags. Perpignan had in fact been involved in a crucial game that weekend in the European Cup. Sadly, they had lost. M.Oliver did not show his disappointment and was very jolly and effervescent. By contrast I am sure that had it been me that had suffered this setback in an important soccer game back home I would still have been long faced and in mourning. He took me through the range of flags and banners and was delighted to share his recollections of his many trips throughout Europe in support of his beloved Perpignan. He was the epitome of someone for whom 'it is the taking part that counts'. Not like me.

Before taking us through a leisurely relaxed tasting M.Oliver went over to a large fridge and played up to our English sensibilities. Sure enough on one of the shelves was the ubiquitous foie gras and with just the hint of a knowing smile on his face he offered us this local delicacy. Without waiting for our embarrassed reply he withdrew the offer and brought out a couple of local cheeses for which we were truly thankful. I have reluctantly eaten foie gras a couple of times on our travels through France and I have no intention of adding to those experiences. Monsieur was still chuckling when he returned to the table.

Located just behind him was a smaller fridge and from this he produced a couple of bottles of white wine and a rosé. The striking thing about them was the colourful labels, in the same style that had attracted us in the first instance in Collioure. The first one we tried was a white and it was refreshingly chilled and with some of the local cheese provided by M.Oliver it was a wine perfectly suited to the location. The wines here in Roussillon are not complex but they are fruity and clean on the palate and with the sun beating down they are a perfect complement to the climate of this sun baked land.

The rosé wine on offer is even more suited to the plain on which Mas Deu sits. The label has a print of an artwork by a man named Andreu Jordi whom I believe is an artist from Andorra. It is a painting of a girl and is a little Daliesque. Colourful and striking. This rosé is intensely fruity but not as alcoholic as some of the rosé wines of the Languedoc, particularly the famous names of Lirac and Taval close to Avignon. I know this is only a tasting but we could have finished the bottle and I am sure that Monsieur Claude would have allowed us to do so. French drink driving laws and my conscience would not allow it although there is no way I am wasting any of this nectar by spitting it out. M.Oliver produces a cheesy accompaniment for our pleasure, a little nibble that is not unlike the gougeres you find in Burgundy that are often offered at a degustation. I am not quite sure who is the more chilled of our merry party, ourselves as the tasters or M.Oliver who is clearly enjoying this tasting session as much, if not more than we are.

This domain is unlike ones you will find in the more upmarket wine centres such as Beaune and Chablis for instance. I cannot see a price list, there are no wooden cases set out for you to take home and impress your friends, there are no souvenir add on purchases. M.Oliver loves his wine, he is proud to have produced it and if you want to buy some he is most happy to oblige. If you don't, well he has enjoyed showing it to you anyway and there will always be other customers. His product he knows is excellent and will give the most discerning of wine connoisseurs' complete satisfaction.

After trying his red wine we decide to purchase his rosé and he makes up a case to add to our increasing supplies in the boot of our car. M.Oliver carries it outside and as he does so two other members of the family are returning the ancient tractor from the fields and they smile at us, no doubt knowing that we have bought a case of pure pleasure to be savoured later. M.Oliver firmly shakes my hand and I bid goodbye. Niamh's hand he tenderly takes and bows to give it a gentle kiss. As we drive away down the dusty track we wave from the car and Niamh settles into her seat, her mind taken to another place. What a gentleman.

# CORBIÈRES & MINERVEROIS

The location we were heading back to was the village of Boutenac to our bed and breakfast home for three nights. Sadly, the family no longer offer accommodation as of today but it is in a fine old town house, one that probably belonged to a well to do wine merchant in times past. The property was gorgeous, very sympathetically restored. The furniture was chosen by someone with a fine eye for detail and empathy for the period of the structure. It was a place that I congratulated myself on finding and we spent a wonderful time here. The family were so friendly and welcoming and on the first night offered an evening meal with most of the guests happily accepted the invitation. This was served in the garden under a vaulted tented canopy. As the sun went down on a balmy summers evening the setting was magical. The food was of a standard that complimented the ambiance perfectly and we were very happy in spirit as we made our way back to the sumptuous bedroom.

This evening we had also learnt a little more about the wines of the area and that is always something we are eager to do. Accompanying our meal we had been served a variety of wines from a local domain that I had already researched to a degree before coming to the region. The producer was Château la Voulte-Gasparets 11200 Boutenac. No further address details are necessary as it is a small commune and you cannot miss it. The wines enhancing the meal were superb. White, rosé and the star of the show a sun baked red, typical of the production of this parched land.

The next day we decided to pay a visit to the domaine. Although it is a château the domain is not intimidating and the tasting room is pleasantly compact with glasses arranged on some oak barrels. We can only have a brief look at the cellars that have a high concentration of new oak barrels as you would expect. They also have a storage method that we will see in many areas of France although it is not that common but displays a fine heritage. These storage tanks are set into the stone walls and are accessed for production by a small cast iron door set into the wall. You kind of expect to find a furnace behind the door rather than vats full of wine. It is always fascinating to see the different methods of fermentation and storage employed throughout France. This method of producing the wine benefits from the coolness of the tanks behind the thick stone walls. The welcome is warm and a degustation immediately offered. Patrick et Laurent Reverdy are the sixth generation to have worked the vineyards and consequently have a long history and tradition to uphold. The current custodians of the vineyard are recognized as one of the leading lights of the wine producers of Languedoc- Roussillon and the wine quality testifies to that. The tasting as we always seem to find is generous but despite enjoying the white and rosé it is really the red wine that we are interested in on this visit. It is a wine that could only have been produced in this area, fruity yes, but it is the spice of the land coming through that really grabs your attention. We concur that this will be most enjoyable back home in the middle of a long English winter and so it proves.

Our selection has to be the Volte Gasparet Corbieres Cuvee Reserve 2001. This is a wine that can proudly hold its own in any company and is a superb find. It was even more remarkable that our hosts back at our accommodation should be kind enough to serve this as their house wine with our meal. We were privileged to have had such an experience.

The next day we decide to make our way to Minerve, a place that has its place in history and a focal point for a subject that has always intrigued me – the Cathars and the Crusades against them.

Our first port of call is Homps, a village set alongside the canal du Midi. Homps first came to my attention in one of the English chef Rick Stein's food travel series although to be fair he concentrated on the incongruous shop here that sells solely English food staples. That aside, the setting alongside the canal is beautiful and we took a most enjoyable stroll along the canal, passing a few cafes and restaurants that were tempting us to stay. It is a calm place to stroll and the effect of the boats gently drifting by on the canal is very soothing. It is a place to linger but sadly today our plans will not allow it.

The village has some interesting architecture in the churches and chapels that date back to around the 12$^{th}$ century. These were established around the time of the crusades. One is particularly beautiful - Saint-Michel chapel. It is listed as a historical monument that is built in an exquisitely beautiful Romanesque style. The chapel was erected in the eleventh century by the order of Hospitallers of St. John of Jerusalem and is now a private chapel.

If you stay in the village you have several opportunities to sample the local wines and Homps will not disappoint on that score. This is a fine place to enjoy the Canal du Midi and this beautiful canal you will find has many other picturesque spots along its length as it meanders through the southern landscape. I have still not been on the actual canal but having seen people working the many locks on this canal I feel I should probably continue to enjoy it from the banks and through the lens of my camera.

The road to Minerve winds gently up the valley from the Beziers to Carcassonne road, climbing steeply, then falling into the town of Aigues-Vives, located along the River Cesse. In summer the river disappears underground in this wild landscape of Causses. The landscape is still quite gentle but soon becomes much more dramatic and stark as you reach La Caunette, tucked under a cliff. Either side of the road are delicate stone bridges offering tracks leading up to perched farmhouses. Carrying on past all of these the road to Minerve becomes ever more dramatic. As you round one of the many corners Minerve appears in front of you, a miraculous village perched over a convergence of rivers. It is perched over and around deep gorges. Minerve is a wonderful survivor, many terrible deeds having taken place here including the massacre inflicted by Simon de Montfort during the Cathar crusades in 1210.

I have long been fascinated by this region and the history of the Crusades. I struggle to comprehend how with the claimed backing of God and the urging of the Pope these men could behave in such a manner, performing terrible atrocities in a fanatical attempt to rid the land of so called heretics. Simon de Montfort laid a heavy siege to the seemingly impregnable fortress village of Minerve. It ultimately proved not to be impregnable and the method of shortening the siege was to attack St Rustique's well, the principal water source for the village.

The village as can be seen even today was for most situations extremely well defended with double surrounding walls, and overhanging ledges. DeMontfort was a determined and cruel opponent and nothing would stop him in breaking any resistance to what was as he saw it – the will of God and the Pope. And as the walls gave in at St Rustique's well, Viscount Guilhem of Minerve negotiated the town's surrender. He saved the local villagers and himself, but around 140 Cathars who had taken refuge in the village were burnt at the stake, because they refused to deny their faith. This was a scene often repeated throughout the region over the next 35 years. This burning of Cathars at Minerve was the first in the crusade.

The Cathars are also referred to as Parfaits, the French word for perfect. These were members rather than clergy of their popular religious movement in Southern France but they were always at odds with Rome. They of course could not be perfect but they believed that the lifestyle they adopted would gain rewards for them, especially in heaven. They were people of abstinence and were viewed as almost angelic because of their way of life.

We parked the car just outside the village by the dramatic arched stone bridge that appears to be the only way into the village itself. The bridge appears as if it may have been built by the Romans as an aqueduct. It is old but not that ancient to be Roman. It is quite a feat of engineering though with its span above the deep ravine in front of the village clinging to the rocky outcrop at the far side. The day was almost unbearably hot at around 40 deg centigrade and it felt a rather long exposed walk over the narrow bridge into the village where at last there was some shelter in the labyrinth of streets.

The fortress of those times is only to be seen in the shape of a small tower but the village is very atmospheric with narrow streets and alleys providing pleasurable detours around the village. There is still a small 12$^{th}$ century church in the village and this is a relaxing place to sit and contemplate the dreadful past of this now peaceful and beautiful location.

Finding a small sheltered courtyard with a café serving light lunches and chilled carafes of rosé wine we settled down for a few quiet moments as the heat of midday passed by. There are not vast amounts to see in the village but the main reason to visit it is for its dramatic position and the views. The restored streets and the old church give a sense of times past but this is a quiet, peaceful place now. As you sit outside the church with the dramatic backdrop of the landscape behind you it does take a leap of imagination to picture the appalling events that were enacted here. There is a small, very simple memorial to the Cathars and their genocide just outside the church. You can see from this vantage point that they may have felt quite secure; the village is high and separated by this deep gorge. They were not safe however and although the structure of the village was spared to some extent the religious people sheltering here met a brutal end. It is a story repeated throughout this region but now we English visitors are warmly welcomed in a way that Simon de Montfort most certainly was not.

In the commune itself there is the wine outlet of Domaine Cavailles, 2 Grand Rue Minerve. They produce a typical red and rosé of the region and you are welcome to have a tasting with them. We actually bought a bottle of the sweet desert wine of the region as we had already decided on our main visit for wine tasting. That domaine would be on the way out of the village a couple of miles away.

The domaine we had decided to pay a call on was Les Trois Blasons who have a caveau at Route d'Olonzac, 34210 Azillanet on the route back to Homps. The domaine is set amongst the vines in a parched landscape of gently sloping land. It is a relatively high vineyard situated at around 300 metres above sea level. This domain is part of a cooperative – Alliance Minervois. The vineyards represented here consist of some 600 winegrowers and stretch from Narbonne to Carcassonne. Here at Azillanet we can try a wide selection of wine, all of which are fine representatives of the particular *terroir* of the various villages. The particular portions of land around Minerve are referred to as Le Causse and the grape varieties are cabernet sauvignon, syrah, chardonnay, sauvignon blanc and merlot. These wines have won many awards and are included in the Guide Hachette and deservedly so. The reds are warm and spicy and we decided to take home a case of the Cuvée Gaïa. Ours was a 2001 vintage. This turned out to be one of the most admired wines by our friends back home in Lancashire and much requested by them at our dining table as a winter warmer. This is a special red from a dramatic and sun baked landscape. I can only feel that had this wine been around at the time of the crusades then just maybe differences could have been settled in a more civilised fashion over a glass or two of this wonderful red.

For those of you with slightly less interest in the fruits of the vine in this region then the cave does host art exhibitions, mainly sculpture. These are changed regularly and are quite eclectic and surprising. I highly recommend a visit here and this whole region is a photography and history lover's dream.

This area has been a delight and a surprise. Most of the time back in England this southern French region is given a pretty bad press as regards the standard of wine production. We have found that not to be the case when seeking out domains for ourselves. The quality has been excellent and also it is a region that can express itself outside the appellation d'origine controlee if it so desires. This concession produces many interesting wines. It is a region where you can truly understand this mysterious French word of *terroir*. The wines created here are the product of the land. The spicy quality of the reds is the expression of the makeup of the sun-baked, parched ground the vines are rooted in. It is here where a fine dedicated producer knows how to use this soil and a visit to this region is a wine lover's delight.

Our stay at Boutenac had come to a close and it was one of the most enjoyable bed and breakfast homes we have visited in France. Madam and Monsieur were delightful hosts and the property itself a sympathetic testament to all things French culture could conjure up. On leaving we were both given some lovely gifts by them and simple though mine was it could not have delighted me more – it was salt from the etangs close to the Mediterranean and would be effectively used to accompany my fish cookery back home in England.

# THERE IS MORE

As I was writing this fourth and planned final book in the series about our travels in France over the last twenty five years I had come to realise that I would not fit all I wanted to write about into four books. I had not even covered Normandy and Brittany and only scratched the surface of Burgundy. In writing about our wine travels it became apparent that in this book I could only cover the early travels and our later visits to Burgundy, the Rhone valley and Provence could only be hinted at. France is a large country and there is so much to discover and we certainly achieved that over the twenty five years of visiting the regions of France. So this may not be the last book. I do hope you have enjoyed my take on touring France and most of all I would wish that my writings will inspire you to travel. These are my personal recollections and these are the people and places we found. You can find so much more that will make your own journey personal and provide life long memories. Off you go!

# DOMAINE ADDRESSES IN BOOK ORDER

**Château de l'Esparrou**, Route de Saint-Cyprien, 66140 CANET EN ROUSSILLON
www.chateau-esparrou.com/

**Cave Tambour**, 136 Bis Avenue du Puig del Mas, 66650 BANYULS-SUR-MER
www.domaine-tambour.com/

**Domaine Servin**, 20 Avenue Oberwesel, 89800 CHABLIS
www.servin.fr

**Domaine Laroche**, 10, rue Auxerroise 89800 CHABLIS
www.larochewines.com

**Alain Geoffroy**, 4 rue de l'équerre 89800 BEINE (Près(near) Chablis)
www.chablis-geoffroy.com

**Dampt Freres**, Chai et Cave de dégustation, 1 rue de Fleys à COLLAN 89700
http://emmanuel.dampt.pagesperso-orange.fr/

**Domaine Bersan**, Jean-Louis & Jean-Christophe, 20, rue du Docteur Tardieux, 89530 SAINT-BRIS-LE-VINEUX
www.bersan.fr

**Domaine Laporte** Cave de la Cresle - Route de Sury en Vaux, 18300 Sancerre, SAINT SATUR
www.laporte-sancerre.com

**Joseph Mellott**, Route de Ménétréol – 18300 SANCERRE
www.josephmellot.com

**de Ladoucette** - Château du Nozet, 58150 POUILLY-SUR-LOIRE
www.deladoucette.fr

**Petit le Brun et Fils**, 10 rue Lombard 51190, AVIZE
www.champagnepetitlebrunetfils.com

**Domaine La Boutinière**, Rue Commandant Lemaître, 84230 CHÂTEAUNEUF-DU-PAPE
www.domainelaboutiniere.fr

**Domaine Lafargue et Fils**, 30126 SAINT LAURENT DES ARBRES
www.earllafargue.e-monsite.com

**Château Redortier**, La Grange Neuve, 84190 SUZETTE

**Domaine de Font-Sane**, 84190 GIGONDAS
www.font-sane.com

**Château Val Joanis**, PERTUIS 84120
www.val-joanis.com

**La Cave de Bonnieux**, Place de la Gare, 84480 BON-

NIEUX

www.cave-bonnieux.com

**Domaine Huet**, 11 rue de la Croix Buisée, 37210 VOUVRAY

www.domainehuet.com

**Bernard Fouquet**, Domaine des Aubuisieres 32 Rue Gambetta, 37210 VOUVRAY

www.vouvrayfouquet.com

**Domaine Bernard Ardois**, 1063, route de Beauval, Roche 41110, SEIGY

**Domaine des Chézelles**, 18 rue du Grand Mont, 41140 NOYERS-SUR-CHER

www.domaine-chezelles-vins-touraine.com

**Camel Valley Vineyards**, Nanstallon, BODMIN, Cornwall, PL30 5LG

www.camelvalley.com

**Domaine Boillot Lucien & Fils**, 1 Rue Docteur Pujo, 21220 GEVREY-CHAMBERTIN

**Domaine Prieur Brunet**, Ch. Perruchot rue de Narosse, 21590 SANTENAY

**Maison Champy**, 5 Rue du Grenier À Sel, 21200 BEAUNE

www.maisonchampy.com

**Château Thivin**, 630 route du Mont Brouilly, 69460 ODENAS www.chateau-thivin.com

**Château de la Saule**, 71390 MONTAGNY-LES-BUXY
www.bourgogne-vigne-verre.com/en/4-chateau-de-la-saule
**Château Fuissé**, 71960 FUISSÉ, Bourgogne
www.chateau-fuisse.fr
**Domaine Roger Luquet**, 101 Rue du Bourg, 71960 FUISSÉ
www.domaine-luquet.com
**Chateau Mas Deu**, 66300 TROUILLAS

**Château la Voulte-Gasparets**, 11200 BOUTENAC
www.lavoultegasparets.com
**Domaine Cavailles**, 2 Grand Rue, 34210 MINERVE
**Les Trois Blasons**, Route d'Olonzac, 34210 AZILLANET
www.allianceminervois.com

The French Travel Series
Available on Amazon –
Free on Kindle Unlimited
First Time We Saw Paris
How a Small French Cafe Changed our Lives
Neal Atherton
Neal Atherton
Thyme for Provence
Lavender, People & Places
NEAL ATHERTON
A DREAM OF PARIS
NEW RELEASE on Amazon
A Personal Paris Travel Memoir

A Bullet for Life
Love
Conflict &
Family Survival
A remarkable family history of love and tragedy unknowingly bringing a family together on the Boer War battlefields of South Africa
The story begins in Spain around 1800 and goes through to Italy 1943
The final modern day twist will amaze and delight you
Neal Atherton
Includes chapter on how the research was done with Ancestry tips to follow

# ABOUT THE AUTHOR

## Neal Atherton

My passion is writing about travel and particularly French travel. I have traveled extensively in France and wine and food has always featured on my travels and now in my books. My friends always await our return from France with the latest new finds from the vineyards and I was more than happy to keep sampling. I am from Lancashire in the north of England but have now relocated to Somerset (nearer to France) and able to enjoy devoting my time to writing and new discoveries.

France came late to me as a destination, in fact so conservative was my travel upbringing that it was a long time before I even ventured to Cornwall. I have more than made up for the slow start and have enjoyed helping many others with their travel plans to France and especially to Paris and Provence.

I have written a series of four books on France - Three are also on Amazon: THE FIRST TIME WE SAW PARIS - about our first steps in French Travel, THYME FOR PROVENCE - our discovery of that glorious region and the people and places we met and discovered, A DREAM OF PARIS - a personal memoir of our times in Paris with friends and immersing ourselves in its culture and history.

I also write about ancestry and genealogy and my first book

about our incredible family story themed around war and the military is now on Amazon - A BULLET FOR LIFE.
I love the English game of cricket, golf, soccer, photography, walking and cooking. Oh, and travel of course.

# PRAISE FOR AUTHOR

*Kindle Edition Verified Purchase re A Dream of Paris*

*'Found this well written and informative. Certainly gets the atmosphere of Paris and especially the gastronomic side of what Paris has to offer'*

- AMAZON

*First Time We Saw Paris*
*5.0 out of 5 stars Delightful*
*Reviewed in the United States on February 1, 2020*
*Format: Kindle Edition Verified Purchase*
*I so enjoyed the style of writing. It felt like I was there with you. It did inspire me with a desire to visit France and these places in particular. I would recommend this book to anyone who is thinking of a trip to France.*

- AMAZON

*5.0 out of 5 stars Enjoyed*
*Reviewed in the United States on April 27, 2020*
*I enjoyed this book so very much. As I read it, I felt like I was sitting with a friend and he was telling me about his trip. The descriptions of the countryside were awesome only outdone by the ones about the food I recommend it and hope you enjoy it as much as I did.*

*Thyme for Provence*
*5.0 out of 5 stars Entertaining and very enjoyable*
*Reviewed in the United States on August 25, 2019*
*Format: Kindle Edition*
*Very much enjoy his stories of his travels through France, this tyme in Provence. These stories always make me want to return to the wonderful French countryside and people.*

*- AMAZON*

# BOOKS BY THIS AUTHOR

## First Time We Saw Paris

Across the channel - a sense of wonder at seeing Paris for the first time - south on Autoroute du Soleil - Catalonia & the Mediterranean Sea - Innocents Abroad.
What did we find - what is France REALLY like?
We found a lifelong love of France BUT first .........
French travel has been fun, we were burgled on our very first night, we discovered the finest cafe that changed our travel lives the very next morning, we learned about French wine, we escaped the most horrendous gite, we found the best of gites, B & B's & people, we laughed and cried with dear friends in Paris, I was hosed down by a crazy owner to 'cool me down' in Provence, our breakfast was served by the French army, we stepped out of our comfort zone and discovered the best of French culture.

The experiences are many and varied and this is the first of four travel memoirs that tell the full story - PROVENCE is next - Please be with me from the start. - Please use the LOOK INSIDE feature

I will inspire you to find the most amazing places & people yourself in this wonderful land

For me it has been the most remarkable ride for a very reluctant traveller - Come with me

## Thyme For Provence

'Monsieur, vous êtes très chaud du voyage

- you are hot from the journey, oui?'
I could only agree that I was indeed the very picture of the Englishman in the noonday sun.
She broke away from watering her extensive and beautiful enclosed garden.
'I will cool you down'
Turning the hose on my fully clothed self she most certainly did that.

This is an affectionate account of our French travels in Provence - meeting so many remarkable (and eccentric) people and places over a 20 year period travelling by car from the North of England
Is it a guide book? Well, the people and places are there but I really want to inspire you to make your own journey and treasure this gorgeous region.
If not, then be entertained from your armchair and let your imagination take you to the lavender fields in a great summer read

## A Dream Of Paris

Is Paris More Beautiful in the Rain?

This is a personal memoir of our times spent in Paris and our love of this endlessly absorbing city and its people.
I recall many travels with friends, finding restaurants & cafes and enjoying the sights and sounds of Paris.
I travel in the footsteps of Hemingway and enrich the writing with the history and art the city has produced.
My fascination with how the city and its people were affected by the Occupation and eventual liberation in August 1944 and how that personally affected me. I face the challenge of returning to find out how Paris recovers from the appalling events of the night of the Bataclan attacks.

The theme of the film 'Midnight in Paris' threads through the strolls through Paris and 'Is Paris more beautiful in the rain?' I have not set it out to be a guidebook but it will inspire you to follow my footsteps but most of all make you dream of Paris and to visit making your own memories.

## A Bullet For Life

Kimberley, South Africa - 1900
Saturday February 10th 1900 was another day under siege for James Atherton. He was serving with the Loyal North Lancashire Regiment engaged in defending Kimberley in South Africa and urgently in need of relief which came five days later. His friend on duty next to him was Samuel Hall from Preston in Lancashire, a town some 11 miles from James home in Darwen. The following day Samuel would be dead.
The friends had travelled to fight as professional soldiers together twelve months earlier and Samuel may also have been with James in Ceylon on his previous posting. The death of Samuel was a crushing blow to James but on his return he visited Samuel's widowed mother Sarah now also living in Darwen. Sarah was born in Lisburn in Ireland and had settled with her husband William, a man from County Cork, now an Army pensioner.
It was here that he found love amongst the tragedy. Samuel's sister Lydia was 22 and they were married some two years later.


Did Lydia know of James troubled past?


Let us see but the ending returns to South Africa, via Spain, Cornwall, Cumbria, Ireland, France, Italy and Lancashire and spans two centuries - The ending is heartwarming in the most unexpected coming together of a family line in an amazing coincidence - Life truly does hang by a thread - or a bullet

This a story that has taken some 12 years of research and although it was fun to unravel all the complex details it was like most family research also at times frustrating and I conclude the book with some research tips that I trust will be helpful.

Printed in Great Britain
by Amazon